THE COMPLETE SYSTEM FOR EQUIPPING LEADERS & MOBILIZING MINISTRY TEAMS

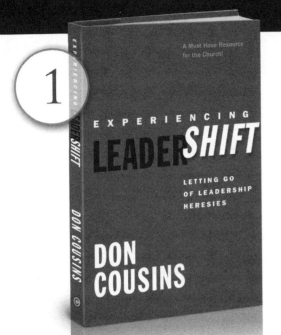

FOR PASTORS AND LEADERS

❶ Experiencing LeaderShift—Applicable for leaders and anyone who wants to participate fully as a member of the body of Christ, this book offers insights into destructive heresies leaders have mistakenly embraced and explains the biblical foundation for leading as God intended.

❷ Experiencing LeaderShift Application Guide—Designed to help turn the vision from *Experiencing LeaderShift* into action, this guide instructs ministry leaders how to better equip others to function as devoted members of the body of Christ. This dynamic guide includes a six-session DVD.

FOR MINISTRY LEADERS AND THEIR TEAMS

❸ Experiencing LeaderShift Together—Aimed at mobilizing church staff, volunteers, and church-ministry team members, these comprehensive guides describe God's plan for His church and the roles of its members. Together, leaders and participants will learn specifically how their efforts can transform their ministry within the body of Christ.

What people are saying about …

"This *Experiencing LeaderShift Application Guide* is **not** another 'How to be a great leader in seven easy steps.' Instead it tackles the tough question of 'Are you a leader?' Every church that longs to equip the saints to do the work of the ministry, but is having the staff do everything, must experience *leadershift*. This Application Guide is also an invaluable tool for evaluating and hiring staff. It has numerous assessments and applications. In my nine years of ministry, I never once asked a person what his or her spiritual gifts or passions were. I didn't take time to put the right people in the right places. It's a little embarrassing to admit that. I hadn't run with confidence and FREEDOM in ministry, until I *experienced* leadershift."

Todd Skinner, young adult pastor at Neighborhood Church, Redding, California

"My encounter with *Experiencing LeaderShift* took the *idea* of becoming an equipping church from a conceptual model to a practical reality. *LeaderShift* gave me practical handles for recognizing and empowering ministry leaders to meaningfully equip their teams. As equipping leaders, our role is to provide the environments, teaching, opportunities, and vehicles to allow people to keep all the gears turning in harmony. *LeaderShift* provides the framework and the applications to train, release, and envision your ministry leaders to join the Holy Spirit in truly fruitful and fulfilling ministry. As one of the pastors on our staff put it, 'I've had years of education, and over fifteen years of pastoral experience—and this is the first time I've ever understood equipping leadership with such clarity.'"

Shawn Andrews, ministry pastor at Daybreak Church, Pennsylvania

"The spiritual growth of God's people is not dependent on the leadership practices of corporate America, or the polity of our church, or having the intimacy of a small congregation or even the resources of a large church. True spiritual growth emerges as we practically implement the thoughts and practices of Jesus in the body of Christ. The *Experiencing Leadershift Application Guide* has been a tremendous tool in reintroducing spiritual gifts as they should be expressed in the local body through equippers and servers. *Experiencing LeaderShift* has been instrumental in changing everything from the way we approach volunteer leadership to staff hiring. Matching spiritual gifts to the role needing to be filled has energized the body to function supernaturally."

Erich Roeh, executive pastor of Neighborhood Church of Redding, California

"*Experiencing LeaderShift* is food for the mind and inspiration for the soul in helping us understand how the church can and should function. However, it is the *Application Guide* that is the conduit between inspiration and reality. In the *Application Guide* all your church leaders will be shown a step-by-step process that produces unity of purpose. No stone is left unturned, and ministry is broken down and then rebuilt in the model that produces spiritual fruit from our church ministries, its leaders, and the ministry servants who are mentored. In the end God is brought positive attention (glory) and the people of the church are built up!"

Barry Carroll, executive pastor of Horizon Christian Church, Valrico, Florida

"We've been using *Experiencing LeaderShift* training and materials for over three years now and are very pleased with their impact on our ministry leaders. Our leaders enjoy the training class and feel equipped for their calling. We now have a common language for leadership that can be heard throughout the church, a way of talking about ministry strategy that bridges the gap between secular leadership theories and the language of biblical faith. We are committed to moving forward using the *Experiencing LeaderShift* materials and are looking forward to the continuing growth and development of this resource."

Pastor Kurt Helmcke and *Elder Pam Bruning,* North Creek
Presbyterian Church, Mill Creek, Washington

"The *Experiencing LeaderShift Application Guide* has shifted my way of thinking. I now have a greater understanding on how to become a successful leader *God's* way. By using God's definition of success, I redefined my ministry based on a biblical model. I now have a firm grasp on how to use my spiritual gifts to equip others for ministry. I plan to use this guide to train all my leaders because I know it will do wonders for them, as it has for me."

Rodney Owens, spiritual formation pastor at Napa First Baptist Church, California

"Would you like your ministry leaders to experience change in their leadership behavior? *Experiencing LeaderShift* renders a powerful wake-up call to church leaders. Our church leadership culture must be addressed apologetically and practically. The remedy proclaimed *shifts* church leaders back to a biblical understanding and practicum of leadership as ordained by God. This work has influenced my ministry and has pointed me back towards biblical truth with transformational effects."

Geoff Thomas, interim pastor at Moab First Baptist Church, Utah

"Early on in my discipleship journey, *my way* of doing ministry looked a lot different from the way *Jesus* did ministry. Now, thirteen years later, my way is finally *shifting* to His. *Experiencing LeaderShift* has been a transforming process. In part, I see *LeaderShift* as a call for the church to pray about being intentional about discipleship. Jesus prayed and intentionally poured his life into others. He has been and will always be the perfect example of how we carry out the Great Commission."

Scott Bircher, Saturday night worship arts coordinator at Covenant United Methodist Church, Greenville, North Carolina

"As executive director in a large United Methodist church, I have embedded this biblical DNA in more than one hundred staff and volunteer leaders over the past five years. The results speak for themselves: a dramatic increase in the effectiveness of existing leaders; greatly improved communication resulting from a common language for ministry; increased staff capacity as team leaders and trainers; practical help moving several staff and lay members to roles that better reflect their gifts; vastly improved systems that have increased the quantity and quality of volunteers; and, most important, a growing spiritual momentum as we have collectively aligned our ministry to God's plan of action for His church. I strongly encourage you to use the *Experiencing LeaderShift Application Guide* for training your church's leadership."

Charlie Halley, executive director of Covenant United Methodist Church, Greenville, North Carolina

"The best thing about *Experiencing LeaderShift* is that it's so practical. It's like somebody finally put the wheels on the leadership-development car. I use it at every level of ministry, whether I'm working with our elder board, staff, or unpaid ministry team leaders. We definitely believe that we're all in this together, working as a team to equip others for ministry."

Tom Cramer, associate pastor at Geneva Presbyterian Church, Laguna Hills, California

"Two things I especially like about *Experiencing LeaderShift*: First, our experienced leaders started thinking outside the box, developed new enthusiasm for their responsibilities, and began to see a better picture of where their ministry fit into the overall scheme of things. Second, this training provides an entirely new way to view and do ministry that alleviates the anxiety inexperienced ministry leaders often have. In the place of that fear, a new energy develops to take on the challenge. You can see it in their countenance, hear it in their voices, and find it in their team members. Now ministry becomes contagious and energizes all who participate."

Dave Carder, assistant pastor of First Evangelical Free Church, Fullerton, California

EXPERIENCING
LEADERSHIFT

EXPERIENCING LEADERSHIFT

A STEP-BY-STEP STRATEGY FOR CHURCH AND MINISTRY LEADERS

DON COUSINS
BRUCE BUGBEE

David C Cook®

transforming lives together

EXPERIENCING LEADERSHIFT APPLICATION GUIDE
Published by David C. Cook
4050 Lee Vance View
Colorado Springs, CO 80918 U.S.A.

David C. Cook Distribution Canada
55 Woodslee Avenue, Paris, Ontario, Canada N3L 3E5

David C. Cook U.K., Kingsway Communications
Eastbourne, East Sussex BN23 6NT, England

David C. Cook and the graphic circle C logo
are registered trademarks of Cook Communications Ministries.

The Web site addresses recommended throughout this book are offered as a resource to you. These Web sites are not intended in any way to be or imply an endorsement on the part of David C. Cook, nor do we vouch for their content.

Unless otherwise indicated, Scripture quotations are from the *New American Standard Bible,* © Copyright 1960, 1995 by The Lockman Foundation. Used by permission. Scripture quotations marked nkjv are taken from the New King James Version. Copyright © 1982 by Thomas Nelson, Inc. Used by permission. All rights reserved. Italics in Scripture are the authors' emphasis.

ISBN 978-1-4347-6814-8

© 2008 Don Cousins and Bruce Bugbee
Published in association with the Literary agency of Wolgemuth & Associates, Inc.

The Team: Terry Behimer, Thomas Womack, Amy Kiechlin, Jaci Schneider, and Karen Athen
Cover Design: The DesignWorks Group, David Uttley
Interior Design: Boswell Idea Group

Printed in the United States of America
First Edition 2008

1 2 3 4 5 6 7 8 9 10

061608

And He gave some as apostles, and some as prophets, and some as evangelists, and some as pastors and teachers, for the equipping of the saints for the work of service, to the building up of the body of Christ.

Ephesians 4:11–12

CONTENTS

Part Three: Doing Ministry Together

Appendix: Getting More

FROM THE AUTHORS

Our hope is that this *Experiencing LeaderShift Application Guide* will help you fulfill your calling as a leader who equips others for the work of service.

In many churches, ministry leaders tend to function and be evaluated as *program planners* and *event coordinators*. They've been assigned to "lead" a group of people by running a "program" that meets the needs of those who attend. Many do it very well.

Typically, people in the church know they *should* serve. Most of them really *want* to serve. But few know *where* and *how* they can best serve. That's why we coauthored the *Network* process. More than a million people have been served and are now serving others through the discovery of their God-given ministry passions, spiritual gifts, and personal style.

But we see a rising problem. Leaders must make a *shift*.

Before identifying their gifts and passions, volunteers often go to a ministry leader and say, "How can I serve?" A leader might say, "Here are four things we need help with. Pick one." Knowing they should serve and wanting to serve, they pick the area where they feel the most comfortable. Sometimes it works out, but most often it doesn't, because what they agreed to do is not a good fit with their interests (passion), abilities (spiritual gifts), and personality (style). They lack competence and motivation.

When volunteers discover their ministry passions and spiritual gifts, they no longer are uninformed about how they've been created and called to serve. When they now approach a ministry leader, they don't ask, "How can I serve?" Rather, they start by sharing with the ministry leader who they *are*. They communicate what they understand *their* passion to be and how *they* would like to be involved with a team of people committed to similar things. They share what spiritual gifts they feel God has specifically given them. They indicate their personal style and how they can best relate to others. This self-understanding is what now gives them motivation, competence, and authenticity.

But here's what happens in too many churches. A volunteer shares his or her passion, gifts, and style, only to have the leader respond, "That's nice, but these four things are what we really need help with. Pick one." Such a response might have seemed helpful back when the volunteer was uninformed about his or her own passion and gifts. But now it's offensive.

Ministry leaders need to discover their own gifts and passion, and then learn to equip others as indicated in Ephesians 4:11–16. They must lead and organize ministry to reflect God's design for His people, His church, and His mission in the world.

This Application Guide is about moving ministry leaders from primarily program planning and event coordinating to *people equipping*. It's providing the leadership steps necessary for *calling, connecting, coaching,* and *changing* a successful ministry team to have faithful, fruitful, and fulfilled people who are making God famous. This requires a *shift*.

Note: We strongly encourage you to read the book *Experiencing LeaderShift* before launching into this material. *Experiencing LeaderShift* provides the foundation for the implementation strategy in this Application Guide. It presents a thorough, biblical framework for equipping leaders and is filled with real-life illustrations and examples.

Turning Vision into Action

The *Experiencing LeaderShift Application Guide* has been designed to help turn a vision for equipping others into action. It's intended to help you achieve these specific objectives:

- Dramatically increase the effectiveness of existing leaders.

- Train every leader to function as an equipper.

- Establish a biblical model of ministry (and move away from the institutional model).

- Create appropriate spans of care, so everyone is trained, valued, and nurtured.

- Make team ministry a way of life.

- Provide your church or ministry with a leadership development plan and strategy.

- Train leaders to "put more in than they take out" of those they lead.

- Give everyone in your church or ministry a vision of what it means to be faithful, fruitful, and fulfilled in a ministry that makes God famous.

- Raise up more leaders.

- Apply the instruction found in Ephesians 4:11–12—so Ephesians 4:13–16 becomes a reality.

May you discover and walk in the zone of God's anointing through your life and ministry.

—Don Cousins and Bruce Bugbee

INTRODUCTION

First, watch the introductory segment titled "Leader's Intro" on the DVD.

So, you've agreed to take on some leadership responsibilities. Congratulations!
Now what?

- What does it mean to be a leader in the cause of Christ?

- What is God calling you to do?

- What are the biblical principles of leadership you need to adopt and apply?

- How will you equip others for their participation in the work of God's kingdom?

- How does your calling serve and support the mission of your church and the kingdom of God as a whole?

If you're not sure, that's okay. Most people step into positions of leadership without a solid biblical understanding of what they are supposed to do. You, too, need to be equipped, in order to be able to equip others.

The *Experiencing LeaderShift Application Guide* will guide you through some important understandings about God's plan for equipping His church. You'll then apply the equipping process to others through *calling, connecting, coaching,* and *changing.*

Finally, you'll discover how to manage the personal transitions and organizational changes being made.

We strongly recommend that you first read the book *Experiencing LeaderShift*. You'll find references to it throughout this guide. It will provide biblical understanding and real-life illustrations about the principles and applications you'll be working through in the *Experiencing LeaderShift Application Guide*.

We're aware that many elements go into the making of an effective leader. We haven't attempted to address all of them here. The *Experiencing LeaderShift Application Guide* has been designed to assist you in fulfilling your biblical role. The strength of your walk with Christ is foundational for a faithful, fruitful, and fulfilling life and ministry. We trust you're in a right relationship with God and others.

Our purpose is to serve and support you as an equipping leader, so that those you serve will also enjoy a faithful, fruitful, and fulfilling ministry that makes God famous. The *Experiencing LeaderShift Application Guide* has been designed to help you succeed as a leader. You'll see God's strategy for building the church and your unique role within it.

Your time and resources are a stewardship we take seriously. That's why this guide has been designed to provide you with the most challenging applications of biblical truth. We trust your heart for God will be deepened, your equipping gifts will be sharpened, and your passion for the kingdom of God will grow.

This guide has been intentionally designed to integrate your learning and assist your application. A variety of values have been interwoven and embedded into the material.

- *Purpose:* The *Experiencing LeaderShift Application Guide* has been designed to help ministry leaders faithfully fulfill their role in the body of Christ. For this to occur, you must carry out the work of equipping others for the work of service (Eph. 4:12). This is at the heart of God's strategy to build His church. Our intention and prayer is that you, as a ministry leader, will be faithful, fruitful, and fulfilled in your role, so that God becomes famous through your life and ministry.

- *Involvement:* The depth of your involvement depends on you. You can quickly read through the material, pick up some new language and a few ideas, yet never truly change the way you lead. However, if you work through this Application Guide, writing out your thoughts and responding to each of the exercises, you'll *experience* a shift. We believe you'll grow as a leader and become more effective in equipping others. You'll have greater impact, personally and organizationally. A thorough investment in this material over the coming weeks and months will pay dividends for the rest of your life. This is our prayer for you.

- *Pace:* This guide has been structured so you can move through it *at your own pace*. We cannot emphasize strongly enough the importance of working through all the content. Whether you do this individually, with another ministry leader, or as an entire leadership team, pace yourself. You'll be blessed—and those you serve will receive that blessing and be able to be a blessing to others.

- *Success: Experiencing LeaderShift* is designed to help leaders experience biblical success. Being faithful, fruitful, and fulfilled in your role will pave the way for others to become faithful, fruitful, and fulfilled in their roles.

- *Motivation:* We believe you want to "walk in a manner worthy of the calling with which you have been called" (Eph. 4:1). We trust you're convinced that you're "His workmanship, created in Christ Jesus for good works, which God prepared beforehand that we would walk in them" (Eph. 2:10). And we believe you want to "run in such a way that you may win" (1 Cor. 9:24), knowing that "He who began a good work in you will perfect it until the day of Christ Jesus" (Phil. 1:6). So, let's walk together and walk worthy.

How to Use This Application Guide

The *Experiencing Leadershift Application Guide* is intended for leadership training and ministry development. It's for all who are in a leadership role, whether paid or volunteer, whether you lead three people, thirty, or three thousand. It's about assisting all those who have leadership responsibilities in a church, parachurch, or Christian organization.

You can work through these materials in one of two ways (for more details on these options, go to Getting More, section A on page 209):

1. *Self-study:* This approach allows you to personally increase your effectiveness as a ministry leader. This guide has been designed to help you easily work through it on your own.

2. *Leader-led:* This guide is also designed for use by church and parachurch leaders to train current and future ministry leaders. It will provide a powerful support and team-building experience among leaders as you work together as a team through the principles of *Experiencing LeaderShift.*

The following chart will give you some basic time frames for using the Application Guide. Use it to plan your personal schedule or meeting times. Each session has two parts followed by Next Steps. You can work through a complete session and then do your Next Steps, or complete part 1 and do part 2 the next time followed by Next Steps. You have flexibility.

Each part has a DVD segment, Reflection, and Application Zone.

Here are some approximate times.

Session	Part 1	Part 2	Total	Next Steps
1	45	20	65	60
2	40	40	80	60
3	35	30	65	90
4	30	30	60	30
5	45	25	70	90
6	35	60	95	20

In this Application Guide you'll find a variety of components to assist your journey through *Experiencing LeaderShift*:

 # DVD

When you see this icon, start your DVD. There are *two* DVD teaching segments for each of the six sessions. Here you'll find specific instruction, key leadership elements, insights, and testimonies—and all are necessary and integral parts of this guide. The DVD isn't optional, but critical to your learning and application of the equipping process. These teaching segments set up the important work to be done in the application zones.

 # Reflections

These are questions for you to stop and ponder. Don't miss these opportunities to respond and journal how God is speaking to you.

 # Application Zone

After each DVD segment you'll find an Application Zone centered around exercises to help you actually *apply* what you've been learning. This is your connection between information and application. Don't skip over it. Remember, you must be *experiencing* leadershift—and these application zones will help you do just that.

 Next Steps

At the end of each session, you'll find additional applications under the heading Next Steps. They're to be completed before you continue on to the next session. Each one will take from thirty to ninety minutes to complete.

Fork in the Road

We recognize that each participant comes to *Experiencing LeaderShift* from a different place and understanding. So, at various points along the way you'll find directions for getting more in-depth information and help by turning to the Getting More section at the back of this guide. The additional content there is intended to provide you a broader understanding of critical concepts that you may not be as familiar with. (Even if you don't feel the need for this additional information when you reach a Fork in the Road, take a quick peek at it, just for future reference.)

 Getting More

As explained above, you'll be directed to the additional content in the Getting More section when you reach a Fork in the Road. You'll also find all the Getting More content on the DVD in a PDF downloadable file. Go to the Menu / Downloads and find the title of the section you're looking for. Just click to download, and make additional copies as needed.

Downloads

In addition to the Getting More content, we've also put some of the application exercises on the DVD in a PDF downloadable file to print out for future use. Go to the Menu/Downloads and find the title of the section you're looking for. Just click to download, and make additional copies as needed.

(R) References

You'll find references in the Application Guide to several resources that will further enhance your learning and develop your leadership understanding.

Some of these resources include

- *Experiencing LeaderShift,* a book by Don Cousins

- *Experiencing LeaderShift Together,* a curriculum for ministry teams and small groups by Don Cousins and Bruce Bugbee

- *Network,* a seminar process by Bruce Bugbee and Don Cousins

- *What You Do Best in the Body of Christ,* a book by Bruce Bugbee

- *Discover Your Spiritual Gifts the Network Way,* a book by Bruce Bugbee

- *Walking with God,* a small group series by Don Cousins and Judson Poling

Part One
BIBLICAL FOUNDATIONS

Jesus teaches us that foundations are critically important. The wise build their houses on the rock, while the foolish build theirs on the sand. When both houses experienced the same wind, rain, and flooding, the house built on sand was wiped out, while the house built on the rock prevailed. What you build on makes a difference (Matt. 7:24–27).

Jesus identifies these builders for us: The foolish are those who hear His words but don't act on them; the wise are those who not only hear the words of Jesus, but act on them.

Let's be wise.

In part 1, we'll spend the first two sessions looking at the biblical foundations for ministry leadership. While there are plenty of seminars and books about leadership, many are based on business models and institutional thinking, and most fail to make clear the core biblical teaching on leadership in the church. Those that do articulate biblical leadership principles don't get to the application level needed for ministry leaders in our churches.

That's why in this *Experiencing LeaderShift Application Guide* we'll explore "The Leadershift We Need to Make" (session 1) and "God's Plan for Equipping His Church" (session 2). These two sessions lay out the biblical foundations for the equipping process presented in part 2.

THE LEADERSHIFT WE NEED

If you haven't already done so, be sure to view the "Leaders" segment on the DVD, and read through the content in "How to Use This Application Guide" in the introduction.

This first session contains critical truths for understanding biblical leadership, biblical success, and the zone of God's anointing, which are essential for effective ministry.

Remember, your ultimate Application Guide is the Holy Spirit (John 16:13). Pray that you can hear His voice and follow His leading.

 ## DVD: Watch Session 1, Part 1   8 minutes

We need to make a number of leadership adjustments before we can develop equipping leaders and embrace gift-based, passion-driven ministry teams. In particular, two significant shifts are required.

Shift One

Get the right people in the right places for the right reasons at the right time.

Church leaders need to …

- provide a vehicle for understanding and implementing gift-based, passion-driven ministry.

- assist people in gaining a better understanding of what the church is, how it works, who they are, and how they fit in.

We created *Network* to help accomplish this first shift. Other vehicles also are available to assist you.

Shift Two

Get leaders to see themselves as equippers and to function accordingly.

Church leaders need to …

- provide a vehicle for leaders to identify and place equippers in equipping roles and servers in serving roles—through gift-based, passion-driven ministry teams. (For further understanding of this, be sure to read the book *Experiencing LeaderShift*.)
- assist believers and churches to function in the zone of God's anointing by being faithful, fruitful, and fulfilled.

The *Experiencing LeaderShift Application Guide* is primarily about this second shift.

The Zone of God's Anointing

The "zone of God's anointing" is the place of God's presence and power in your ministry—the place where the Holy Spirit flows into and through your life.

In this zone, there's always a reflection of your spiritual gifts and God-given passion under the anointing of the Holy Spirit.

As a leader, you need to be operating in the zone of God's anointing. Then you can also help those following you to identify the zone of God's anointing in their lives.

Can I Lead without the Spiritual Gift of Leadership?

There's a significant emphasis and expectation in the church that pastors and ministry leaders *must* have the spiritual gift of leadership if they're to be effective and successful. Yet a Barna

Experiencing LeaderShift, chapter 1

Research survey indicates that only 8 percent of today's pastors identify *leadership* as a primary spiritual gift.[1]

How can someone lead without the gift of leadership? As a pastor or ministry leader, you may have asked that question and personally felt some tension or struggle.

The truth is, God has given us more than one spiritual gift to provide leadership for the church.

There is a *gift* of leadership, as mentioned in Romans 12:

> Since we have gifts that differ according to the grace given to us, each of us is to exercise them accordingly: if prophecy, according to the proportion of his faith; if service, in his serving; or he who teaches, in his teaching; or he who exhorts, in his exhortation; he who gives, with liberality; *he who leads, with diligence;* he who shows mercy, with cheerfulness. (Rom. 12:6–8)

Then there are the equipping gifts that have a leadership *effect,* as taught in Ephesians 4:

> And He gave some as *apostles,* and some as *prophets,* and some as *evangelists,* and some as *pastors and teachers,* for the equipping of the saints for the work of service, to the building up of the body of Christ. (Eph. 4:11–12)

There are more gifts involved in providing leadership than just the gift of leadership. The gifts of apostleship, prophecy, evangelism, teaching, and shepherding are also part of leading and equipping His followers to do the work of service. Each of these has a leadership effect. At the heart of biblical leadership is the work of *equipping.*

Experiencing LeaderShift is based on the biblical truth that leadership in the church is provided by more people than just those with the specific *gift* of leadership. Leadership also

---

[1] The Year's Most Intriguing Findings, From Barna Research Studies," The Barna Group. December 17, 2001. http://Barna.org/.

comes through those who possess any of the five gifts listed in Ephesians 4:11, as they work to equip others for the work of service (4:12).

Experiencing LeaderShift, chapter 3

Defining Success Biblically

How you define success in your ministry will influence the way you lead.

Based on biblical instruction, a few key components comprise the essence of success in God's eyes—and someone who is successful in ministry will manifest all of them.

- *Faithful:* This means doing what God has called you to do, utilizing all that He has given you to do it. God wants to say to us, "Well done, good and faithful servant" (Matt. 25:21 NKJV).

- *Fruitful:* God wants us to "bear much fruit," as Jesus tells us, "and so prove to be My disciples" (John 15:8).

  The evidences of fruitfulness include

  —*Christlike character,* as seen in "the fruit of the Spirit," which is "love, joy, peace, patience, kindness, goodness, faithfulness, gentleness, self-control" (Gal. 5:22–23).

  —*Christlike influence,* as exemplified in the life of Jesus: "You know of Jesus of Nazareth, how God anointed Him with the Holy Spirit and with power, and how He went about doing good and healing all who were oppressed by the devil, for God was with Him" (Acts 10:38). "And Jesus kept increasing in wisdom and stature, and in favor with God and men" (Luke 2:52).

- *Fulfilled:* God desires to fill us with a sense of esteem, value, and significance. He wants us to experience *joy.* Jesus said, "These things I have spoken to you so that My *joy* may be in you, and that your *joy* may be made full" (John 15:11).

This joy flows from faithful and fruitful ministry—like those whom Jesus sent out into ministry and who then "returned with *joy.*"

• *Making God Famous:* True success brings God glory. When people see our good deeds, they will glorify God (Matt. 5:16). That's why we're to fully exercise our spiritual gifts: "so that in all things *God may be glorified* through Jesus Christ, to whom belongs the glory and dominion forever and ever. Amen" (1 Peter 4:10–11).

 ## Reflections

5 minutes

1. What did you identify with most as Don talked about the "zone of God's anointing"?

_____

_____

_____

2. What is your initial reaction to the explanation about the gift of leadership and the equipping gifts that have a leadership effect (Eph. 4:11)? Would you agree or disagree with this conclusion? Why?

_____

_____

_____

3. If you focused more fully on the biblical definition of success, what's one thing that would need to change in your thinking or practice?

_____

_____

_____

Application Zone

As you think about this vital distinction between (a) the spiritual *gift* of leadership and (b) those who have a leadership *effect* through an equipping gift, here are a few more important considerations:

The Leadership Gift and Equipping Gifts

In Romans 12:8, Paul makes it clear that some have been positioned by the Holy Spirit to lead. Leadership, of course, expresses itself in different ways. Just because someone has the gift of leadership doesn't mean he or she is doing the work of *equipping*.

Having the ability to draw people together and organize them to accomplish a given objective (which is leadership) doesn't mean that you've equipped anyone along the way. Motivated them? Yes. Organized them? Yes. Equipped them? Not necessarily.

For example, leading people on a fishing trip isn't the same as equipping them with the skills to catch fish, or having them lead a fishing trip on their own. In the same way, leading people on a ministry team isn't necessarily the same as equipping them for ministry.

The gifts listed in Ephesians 4:11 are given for the purpose of equipping others. Sometimes one or more of these gifts is coupled with the gift of leadership. The result of this gift-mix is that not only are people led, but they're also equipped for the work of service. At other times, these gifts are expressed *apart* from the specific gift of leadership. The result is still the same—people are equipped for the work of service. In every instance where equipping is taking place, leadership is being provided.

This leadership effect happens when equipping gifts are expressed as God intended. Ministry leaders (and every follower of Christ) can be faithful, fruitful, and fulfilled even when they don't score high for the spiritual gift of leadership.

Simply put, leaders are those who have followers. If you're equipping others for the work of service through the gifts God has given you, you're a leader!

Biblical Success

Work through the following two assessments to help you measure both your *personal* and *ministry* success.

Personal Success

Are You Being Faithful?

1. What has God called you to? What contribution have you been called to make to the body of Christ? Be as specific as you can.

   _____

   _____

   _____

2. What has God equipped you with in order to be faithful? What has He given you—what gifts, passions, resources, skills, experiences?

   _____

   _____

   _____

3. To what degree do you feel faithful? (Circle one.)

   a. I feel *unfaithful*—I'm *not* using what God has given me; I'm *not* fulfilling God's call.

   b. I feel *somewhat faithful*—I'm using *some* of what God has given me.

   c. I feel *faithful*—I'm using what God has given me to fulfill His calling.

   d. I feel *completely faithful*—I'm using *all* God has given me to accomplish His calling for my life.

   Express your feeling about this in your words.

   _____

   _____

   _____

   _____

   _____

Are You Bearing Fruit?

4. Describe your Christlike character—the fruit that's evident *within* you. (For this, you may want to evaluate yourself according to the fruit of the Spirit listed in Gal. 5:22–23.)

_____

_____

_____

_____

5. Describe your Christlike influence—the fruit that's being manifested *through* your life. (See Christ's example in Acts 10:38.) Be specific.

_____

_____

_____

_____

Are You Experiencing Fulfillment?

6. To what degree do you feel fulfilled? (Circle one.)

   a. I feel *unfulfilled*—my role isn't satisfying.

   b. I feel *somewhat fulfilled*—some days yes, some days no.

   c. I feel *fulfilled*—my role is very satisfactory.

   d. I feel *overflowing*—overwhelmed with joy.

7. In what times and circumstances do you feel most fulfilled in your ministry?

_____

_____

_____

_____

Are You Making God Famous?

8. In what ways is God becoming famous through your life? Be specific.

_____

_____

_____

_____

Increasing Your Personal Success

9. Look back over your answers to the previous questions. What are the implications here regarding your *success*?

_____

_____

_____

_____

10. What adjustments or changes do you want to make in light of this exercise?

_____

_____

_____

_____

Now that you've assessed your personal success, it's time to turn your attention toward the ministry you lead. The following worksheet will point you in the right direction.

Ministry Success

Are Your People Being Faithful?

1. List the people or groups under your leadership who are being faithful in their ministry positions. Who is making a faithful contribution based on what God has given them?

    _____

    _____

    _____

2. Now list the people or groups under your leadership who are *not* currently ministering in a faithful way.

    _____

    _____

    _____

Are Your People Bearing Fruit?

3. What fruit do you see being manifested *in* and *through* the lives of the people you lead?

    _____

    _____

    _____

4. In what specific ways has God used you to equip them to "bear much fruit" (John 15:8)?

    _____

    _____

    _____

Are Your People Experiencing Fulfillment?

5. Which of the following descriptive phrases best describes the people under your leadership, in regard to their ministry? (Circle one.)

    a. They feel *unfulfilled*—their role isn't satisfying.

    b. They feel *somewhat fulfilled*—some days yes, some days no.

    c. They feel *fulfilled*—their role is very satisfactory.

    d. They feel *overflowing*—overwhelmed with joy.

6. Under each of these terms, list the specific names of people under your leadership who fit that description in regard to their ministry.

Unfulfilled

_____

_____

_____

Somewhat fulfilled

_____

_____

_____

Fulfilled

_____

_____

_____

Overflowing

_____

_____

_____

Are Your People Making God Famous?

7. In what ways is your team serving to make God famous? Be specific.

_____

_____

_____

_____

Our hope is that these two assessments have helped you identify where you're experiencing success and what adjustments might be needed to increase your faithfulness, fruitfulness, and fulfillment.

Next we'll explore how we need to structure our ministries and churches for success.

 # DVD: Watch Session 1, Part 2   8 minutes

The *context* around our leadership makes a difference as we try to make those two significant shifts mentioned earlier:

> *(1) Get the right people in the right places for the right reasons at the right time.*
> *(2) Get leaders to see themselves as equippers and to function accordingly.*

The way churches are structured and function can keep them from experiencing the level of success God desires.

Two Basic Ministry Structures

Every church has some sort of board, a staff, a congregation, and the unbelieving community in which it is located.

In the way all these interact, most churches function along one of two structures—the *institutional* or the *biblical.*

The following chart shows the differences:

Experiencing LeaderShift, chapter 6

Institutional Structure	Biblical Structure
Board *Led* • The board focuses primary attention on matters of administration (facilities, finances, personnel, etc.). • Board members have significant decision-making authority with minimal ministry-leading responsibility.	**Board *Protected*** • The board is responsible for the ministry of the Word and prayer (Acts 6:1–7). • Members are responsible to preserve the unity and purity of the church (Heb. 13:17). • They're accountable for the church's influence—fulfillment of the Great Commission (Matt. 28:19–20) through the Great Commandment (Matt. 22:37–38).
Staff *Serving* • The staff plans programs and coordinates events to meet the needs of the congregation. • The staff has significant responsibility for the work of ministry (leading their program) with minimal decision-making authority.	**Staff *Led*** • The staff is responsible to equip the saints for the work of service (Eph. 4:11–12). • Staff members have appropriate authority and responsibility, with accountability.
Congregation *Served* • The congregation focuses on having its own needs met. • Members respond as consumers and critics of the board and staff.	**Congregation *Serving*** • The congregation contributes to the work of service through gift-based, passion-driven ministry (Eph. 4:11–12; 1 Cor. 12:1).
World *Ignored* • Those outside the church are unaffected and disinterested.	**World *Served*** • As recipients of the church's service, those outside the church find God in and through the body of Christ (John 13:35; Luke 10:30–37; Matt. 28:19–20).

Programs and Values

All ministries, churches, and organizations are structured around *programs* and *values*.

Programs ...

- speak to a specific audience.

- focus on a specific need.

- last for a specific season.

For example, the children's program is, obviously, for children, addressing their needs while they're still young. When they're no longer children, that program's no longer for them. The same is true of the singles program, the youth ministry, a new believers' class, etc. Such programs in the church serve many good purposes.

Values, on the other hand …

- are *not* audience-specific, need-specific, or season-specific.

- are aspects of truth that are *always* true for *everyone.*

If something is a value, it's equally true for a man as for a woman, for a single person as for a married couple, for a seven-year-old as for a seventy-year-old, and for a staff person as for a congregation member.

Values are for all ministry programs. If your church's values include prayer, commitment to biblical truth, giving, and fellowship, then those values should be evidenced in every ministry program in your church.

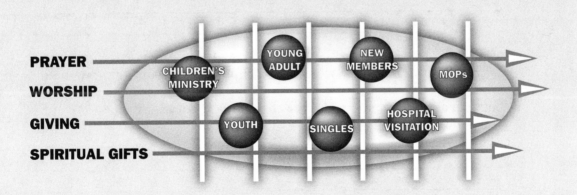

Implementing a value is different from implementing a program.

Experiencing LeaderShift is *not* a program for your church. It's designed to help you implement the *value* of gift-based, passion-driven ministry within a framework of biblical leadership.

 # Reflections

Review the chart comparing the institutional structure with the biblical structure as you answer the following questions:

1. In what ways does your church or ministry function as an institution?

   _____

   _____

   _____

2. In what ways does your church or ministry function biblically?

   _____

   _____

   _____

3. In what ways does your church or ministry's current structure (institutional or biblical) either support or frustrate you (or both)?

   _____

   _____

   _____

4. As a ministry leader, why would it be important for you to know the difference between a ministry *program* in the church and a *value* of the church?

   _____

   _____

   _____

Note: These are good questions to discuss with your team.

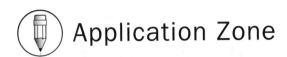 Application Zone   `5 minutes`

Ministry Structures and the People Factor

People are unpredictable and don't always respond as we think they should. You need to allow for this "people factor" when you create a process for people development. Every plan works on paper, but when you involve people, they often don't behave the way you want them to.

Equipping leaders need to cooperate with the movement and activity of the Holy Spirit in others. They understand that people are *in* process, and therefore need a process.

Experiencing LeaderShift honors people as well as God's plan for ministry. Properly calling, connecting, coaching, and changing your team with wisdom according to the Word of God can minimize disruptions caused by the people factor.

How you set things in order determines the outcome of your efforts. Taking a little more time up front will yield greater ministry benefits down the road. As someone has said, sometimes you have to "slow down in order to go faster."

Prayer and Action

Pause and pray, asking God for His specific guidance. As you're making specific applications of what you've learned in this session, don't miss the insights and leadings the Holy Spirit wants to give you.

Take a moment to talk with the Lord. Acknowledge His lordship over you, over your ministry team, and over the church.

Pray about the action steps He's calling you to take, and be open to His guidance in every way.

You may want to record your prayer here, as well as write out whatever you hear from Him.

_____

_____

_____

_____

This completes session 1. Your Next Steps follow, and are to be completed before starting session 2.

 # Next Steps

60 minutes

Now that you better understand the content of session 1, use these Next Steps for further personal applications.

Be sure to complete these Next Steps before moving on to session 2.

When God Shows Up in Our Leading

We're perhaps inclined to think God shows up equally in every expression of ministry, but both biblical and experiential evidence show otherwise.

For example, while we're all called to extend mercy (Luke 6:36), those with the gift of mercy have a special anointing from the Holy Spirit for such a ministry. In the same way, all of us are called to be able to give a defense of the hope that's within us (1 Peter 3:15), yet we know that those with the gift of evangelism possess a greater power for that ministry. The use of our spiritual gifts is a demonstration of God's power at work, but none of us possesses all of the gifts.

We also know from personal experience that each of us possesses more passion for certain kinds of ministry than we do for others. This passion is God-given and reflects His heart within us. Discovering the place of ministry where God's presence and power are working through you is what we mean by the "zone of God's anointing." It's typical for a person who ministers from this zone to say things like "When I do this, God shows up"; "This ministry flows naturally from my life"; and "I was born to do this!"

God's presence is seen in the passion that we display in ministry involvement. God's power is seen in the energy we bring to it and the fruit borne through it.

It's our hope that through this process you'll not only find and experience the zone of God's anointing personally, but also gain the understanding and wisdom to effectively equip and lead others to do the same.

What You
Do Best in
the Body of
Christ

Leadership in the Zone of God's Anointing

Experiencing LeaderShift, chapter 9

Use this exercise to carefully identify the zone of God's anointing for you as a leader. Take the time you need to prayerfully reflect and respond.

1. What do you understand to be your top three spiritual gifts, and in what ways are you expressing each one?

Spiritual Gift	What It Means	How It's Being Expressed

2. How would you describe your ministry passion?

_____

_____

_____

_____

3. What is your personal style or temperament, according to *Network*, Myers-Briggs, DISC, Strengths Finder, etc.?

_____

_____

_____

_____

4. Ask God to help you bring to mind ten "anointed moments"—ten significant ministry experiences in which you clearly felt the Holy Spirit using you to minister to others. These are situations where you've come away feeling "I was born to do that!"

List these in the space provided, and for each one, describe what you did.

Note: Don't think of "significant" as big or grand. It may have been significant only to you. It may have been a single visit to the hospital, or helping a new believer find biblical answers to his questions, or seeing God use you to help someone use her gifts in ministry for the first time. Whatever it was, what matters is that you sensed God's presence and power flowing through your life.

Experiencing LeaderShift, chapter 9

Ten Anointed Moments

1. _____
_____
_____

2. _____
_____
_____

3. _____
_____
_____

4. _____
_____
_____

5. _____
_____
_____

6. _____
_____
_____

7. _____
_____
_____

8. _____
_____
_____

9. _____
_____
_____

10. _____
_____
_____

5. Look over your list of ten "anointed moments," then answer these questions:

a) How were your *spiritual gifts* present in these moments?

_____

_____

_____

_____

b) How do you see your *passion* in these moments?

_____

_____

_____

_____

c) What patterns do you see in these moments? (For example, perhaps each one involved helping people, fixing something, working with individuals or with groups, building relationships, completing tasks, evangelism, compassion for the hurting, or something else.)

_____

_____

_____

_____

Continue to pray and think about the zone of God's anointing in your ministry—especially regarding areas where you need further understanding and affirmation. The Holy Spirit within you will guide you to the people, experiences, and resources you need to teach and inform you.

You've now come to your first Fork in the Road. At each one, take the path that's best for you.

Fork in the Road

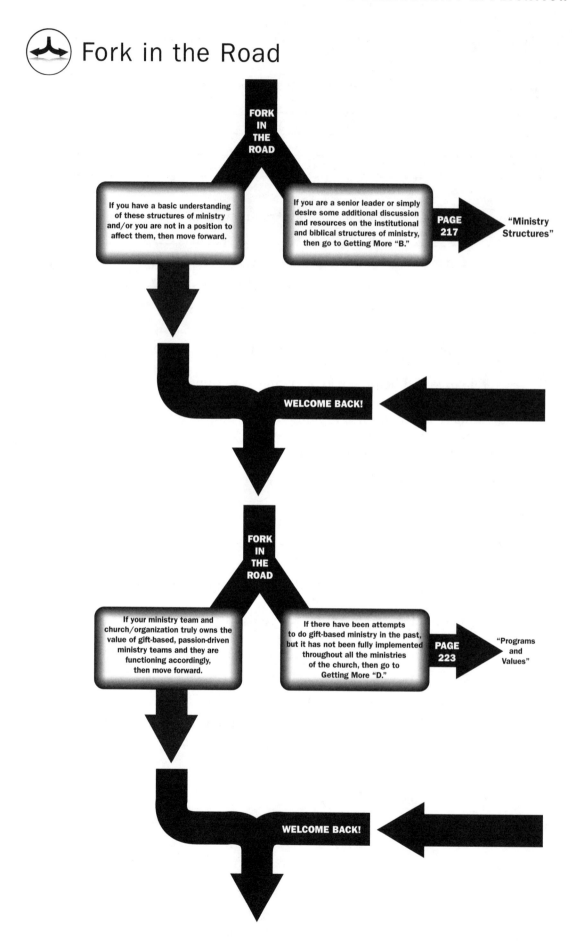

FORK IN THE ROAD

If you have a basic understanding of these structures of ministry and/or you are not in a position to affect them, then move forward.

If you are a senior leader or simply desire some additional discussion and resources on the institutional and biblical structures of ministry, then go to Getting More "B."

PAGE 217

"Ministry Structures"

WELCOME BACK!

FORK IN THE ROAD

If your ministry team and church/organization truly owns the value of gift-based, passion-driven ministry teams and they are functioning accordingly, then move forward.

If there have been attempts to do gift-based ministry in the past, but it has not been fully implemented throughout all the ministries of the church, then go to Getting More "D."

PAGE 223

"Programs and Values"

WELCOME BACK!

GOD'S PLAN FOR EQUIPPING HIS CHURCH

In this session, we'll focus on how to better lead those in your ministry according to equipping and serving.

As we continue building on a biblical foundation, we'll clarify the design God has for His church. We'll see how God has provided the church with both equippers and servers. Each has a specific role, and neither can succeed without the other.

 DVD: Watch Session 2, Part 1 — 9 minutes

Notice again the *equipping* gifts listed in Ephesians 4:11.

> He gave some as apostles, and some as prophets, and some as evangelists, and some as pastors and teachers, for the *equipping* of the saints. (Eph. 4:11–12a).

God has a plan for quipping His church. These "verse-11 people"—the apostle, prophet, evangelist, pastor, and teacher—all make a direct *deposit*. They provide leadership to the body of Christ.

Five gifted roles are mentioned in verse 11:

- apostles—representing the spiritual gift of *apostleship*

- prophets—the gift of *prophecy*

- evangelists—the gift of *evangelism*

- pastors—the gift of *shepherding*

- teachers—the gift of *teaching*

These gifts work in ways that allow God's power to be passed on so that those on the receiving end are equipped to do the work of service. These are the *equipping* gifts, or the *depositing* gifts.

In the next verse—Ephesians 4:12—we're pointed to a larger group of people who are *serving*:

> … for the equipping of the saints *for the work of service*, to the building up of the body of Christ.

"Verse-12 people" make a direct impact—with gifts like mercy, helps, administration, giving, intercession, encouragement, and hospitality, to name a few.

Some are called to *equip;* some are called to *serve;* and both callings are based on *gifts.*

The Problem

When verse-12 people get into a position of leadership and verse-11 people get into a role of serving, there's a problem!

Servers often start a ministry because they're the first to see the need for it. As the ministry grows and more people join them in the work, they can find themselves in a position where they have to equip people (a leadership role).

But there's a reason those verses in Ephesians 4 are ordered as they are.

Equippers are first; they're the leaders.

Servers are the followers, serving on the frontline of ministry.

Both have equal value. Each needs the other to complete their biblical roles.

When *equippers equip* and *servers serve,* the body of Christ works according to God's plan—and as a result, it succeeds.

Confusion

Role confustion comes at a cost.

When servers are in equipping roles

- They see the need, but don't have a vision for the long-term ministry.

- They focus on the need and so don't focus on equipping others.

When equippers are in serving roles

- They can seem critical because they have a vision for how to equip a team.

- They can become a thorn in each other's flesh.

Both equippers and servers are motivated based on their gifting.

 # Reflections

5 minutes

1. Describe the difference between equippers and servers, as you see it.

_____

_____

_____

2. Why is it important that those gifted to equip do so, and those gifted to serve do so?

_____

_____

_____

3. In what ways, if any, are you currently experiencing role confusion, or seeing it in others around you?

_____

_____

_____

Application Zone

All the spiritual gifts fall into one of two categories—*equipping* or *serving*. Every spiritual gift has a unique contribution to make in and through the body of Christ, either to *equip* others for service or to *serve* others directly.

Equipping Gifts

Look again at Ephesians 4:11–12:

> He gave some as apostles, and some as prophets, and some as evangelists, and some as pastors and teachers, for the equipping of the saints, to the building up of the body of Christ.

It's evident from this passage that some spiritual gifts have been given for the purpose of equipping. They focus on three things:

1. Equipping gifts have a leadershift effect.

Take a minute to familiarize yourself with the different equipping gifts.

Role	Spiritual Gift	Their leadership effect tends to be through . . .
Apostle	Apostleship	**... pioneering.** Those with this gift have a divine ability to start ministries and churches, as well as move into new areas, regions, or countries. They're the *entrepreneurs* in the body of Christ.
Prophet	Prophecy	**... revealing.** Those with this gift have a divine ability to speak forth revelation—in keeping with God's Word—to edify, exhort, and comfort others. They're the *revealers* in the body of Christ.
Evangelist	Evangelism	**... proclaiming.** Those with this gift have a divine ability to effectively communicate the gospel to unbelievers so they respond in faith and move toward discipleship. Evangelists are the *reachers* in the body of Christ.
Pastor	Shepherding	**... nurturing.** Those with this gift have a divine ability to nurture, care for, and guide people toward ongoing spiritual maturity in Christ. They're the *relaters* in the body of Christ.
Teacher	Teaching	**... instructing.** Those with this gift have a divine ability to clearly understand, explain, and apply the Word of God, thus causing greater Christlikeness in the lives of their listeners. They're the *educators* in the body of Christ.

2. Equipping gifts are focused on people.

Each of these gifts has a *people focus* (more than a task focus). They're expressed within a context of relationship to others. Equippers are focused on people—their development and ministry success. They want to see those they lead be faithful, fruitful, and fulfilled in order to make God famous through their life and ministry.

3. Equipping gifts are focused on equipping.

While this may seem obvious, it's important to recognize that the five equipping gifts have an *equipping goal.* They develop people from one level of servanthood to the next. They seek to lead people to do the *work of service* they've been created and called to as they grow and mature in Christ.

When saints are being equipped for the work of service, they serve in ways that do something *for* someone else. God doesn't ask us (or need us)

Experiencing LeaderShift, chapter 4

to do anything for *Him*. He's completely self-sufficient as Father, Son, and Holy Spirit. Nothing we do can add to God. However, God sees what we do for one another as an expression of His love working in and through us. The people of God need to be equipped to *do* for one another.

The primary use of an equipping gift (v. 11) is expressed in a way that *prepares* and *trains* someone else to accomplish a task or meet a need in another's life. Equipping leaders make a *deposit* into those they lead. As Ron Gray expressed it, "My fruit grows on other people's trees." That's the heart of an equipper.

Serving Gifts

We observe in Ephesians 4:12 that equipped saints serve one another, thereby building up the body of Christ:

> … for the equipping of the saints for *the work of service,* to the building up of the body of Christ.

It's clear from this verse that many are called to the *work of service*.

A *serving gift* is an expression of God's power through a believer's life that results in the meeting of a need (personally in an individual's life or corporately in a larger setting).

The primary use of a serving gift is expressed in a way so as to directly affect a person or task. Serving gifts have a direct impact in meeting a need. They're *doing* something *for* someone that results in that person being built up.

Serving gifts thus have a different focus from equipping gifts, which are designed to make a *deposit* into a server so the server is effectively equipped to meet needs.

Serving gifts referred to in the New Testament include those listed here:

Serving Gifts	Verse	Those with this gift bring ...
Administration	1 Cor. 12:28	organization and efficiency, thereby increasing effectiveness.
Craftsmanship	Acts 9:36–39	handy skills for designing and building things.
Creative communication	Mark 4:2, 33	creativity and artistic expressions to the community of faith.
Discernment	1 Cor. 12:10	spiritual clarity and divine insights into that which is veiled.
Encouragement	Rom. 12:8	personal affirmation and spiritual motivation that inspires.
Faith	1 Cor. 12:9	confidence, greater trust, hope, and inspiration that seeks to encourage.
Giving	Rom. 12:8	resources, generosity, stewardship, and cheer, propelling the work forward.
Healing	1 Cor. 12:9	God's power, resulting in restoration and wholeness.
Helps	1 Cor. 12:28	needed support and service; manifesting a whatever-it-takes attitude to meet a need.
Hospitality	1 Peter 4:9–10	warmth, acceptance, and relational connection, resulting in another's inclusion.
Intercession	Rom. 8:26–27	protection and spiritual authority and God's intervention through prayer.
Interpretation	1 Cor. 12:10	understanding of spiritual messages which are otherwise indiscernible.
Knowledge	1 Cor. 12:8	awareness of spiritual truths, thereby providing clear direction.
Leadership	Rom. 12:8	vision, direction, and motivation to accomplish an objective.
Mercy	Rom. 12:8	care, compassion, intervention, and advocacy on behalf of those who are weak.
Miracles	1 Cor. 12:10	God's power to bear on otherwise unsolvable circumstances.
Tongues	1 Cor. 12:10	timely spiritual messages of edification.
Wisdom	1 Cor. 12:8	truth and guidance resulting in God-honoring application.

It's clear that equippers (Eph. 4:11) equip servers (v. 12) to serve. God has established this relationship through the gifts of the Holy Spirit for the body of Christ. Not only is this His design; He alone has determined beforehand who will be the equippers and who will be the servers (1 Cor. 12:7, 11, 18). Some people He equips to function primarily as equippers; others He equips to function primarily as servers.

FAQ—Frequently Asked Questions about Equippers and Servers

By now, you're probably asking questions like these:

1. Is equipping more important than serving?

No. The body of Christ needs both equippers and servers equally.

2. Does everyone start out as a server?

Yes. As a matter of maturity, new believers must begin by serving.

3. Can anyone start out as an equipper?

No. New or young believers do not possess the spiritual maturity to equip others.

4. Do we choose our primary function?

No. The Holy Spirit distributes the spiritual gifts (1 Cor. 12:7, 11, 18).

5. What's involved in a person becoming an equipper?

Becoming an equipper requires spiritual maturity, affirmation of gifting, and godly character.

6. Was Jesus an equipper or a server?

He did both: He served the masses, and He equipped the disciples.

7. Can I be both an equipper and a server?

No. You're *primarily* an equipper *or* a server. All of us are called to serve directly on occasion, and all of us are called to equip on occasion. The issue is, what's the focus of my ministry, based on the gifts the Holy Spirit has given me?

8. Can servers develop into equippers?

Yes, if they have equipping gifts. All equippers start out as servers; then, as they mature in Christ and their gifts are affirmed, they develop and function more as equippers. Gifted servers, meanwhile, develop into mature and affirmed servers.

Gifted servers shouldn't try to function primarily as equippers, just as equippers shouldn't try to function primarily as servers. Whether a person is primarily an equipper or a server is a matter of gifting, not role preference. Again, the Holy Spirit distributes the spiritual gifts to each one just as *He* determines (1 Cor. 12:7, 11, 18). So focus on using the gift the Spirit has given you.

Summary

- An *equipper in an equipping position* will primarily identify, attract, develop, and lead individuals and teams so that people are successfully using their spiritual gifts to be faithful, fruitful, and fulfilled in the area of their ministry passion.

- A *server in a serving position* will primarily fulfill the ministry to which God has created and called him or her, successfully ministering directly, personally, or practically by meeting a need, solving a problem, or serving a person or persons.

When There's Confusion

We talked on the DVD about the cost of confusion in ministry roles, and it's appropriate here to add further clarification on this subject.

What happens when an equipper or server is in the wrong position—and why?

When you spot situations like those mentioned below, begin exploring how to resolve them.

1. When *servers* (verse-12 people) are in *equipping* positions:

- They serve to meet needs personally (instead of equipping others to meet needs) …

    because this is what they're gifted, impassioned, and motivated to do.

- The needs of the ministry can eventually overwhelm and burden them …

    because the demands exceed their personal capacity.

- They tend not to attract additional workers to the ministry …

    because their focus is more on meeting needs than on building a team that meets needs.

- They often stifle ministry growth …

because they don't focus on others who can expand it.

- The ministry lacks a great vision …

  because most servers are more "nearsighted" (focused on immediate needs) than "farsighted" (focused on future opportunities).

2. When *equippers* (verse-11 people) are in *serving* positions:

- They stifle ministry growth …

  because they're not in a position to equip others.

- They lack fruitfulness and fulfillment …

  because they aren't doing what comes naturally to them. Their sense of frustration is often felt by others, especially by those in leadership over them.

- Their own development is hindered …

  because they're not focused on what motivates them personally.

- They can become a burden to those in leadership …

  because of the frustration that comes from being wrongly slotted.

You can see the importance of getting the right person in the right position. What about you? Are you primarily an equipper or a server?

Equipper-Server Quotient

Here's an assessment designed to help you discern whether you are primarily an equipper or a server.

Note: Some people tend to rate themselves according to how they think they *should* respond, rather than answering more realistically. This assessment is meant simply as a guide to help you better identify who God has made you to be, and how to more effectively lead and serve accordingly. *The Holy Spirit and the people you serve with will provide you with additional feedback.*

1. Below are seven pairs of statements labeled A and B. For each pair, determine *which statement (A or B) tends to be the truest description of you, most of the time*, and place a check by it.

	A	B	Statement A	Statement B
1			You focus your time and energy on training others to meet needs.	You focus your time and energy on meeting needs personally.
2			Your *primary* ministry goal is developing others so they can serve successfully.	Your *primary* ministry goal is being used by the Lord to meet the needs you see.
3			You think of ministry as an opportunity to involve a variety of people to make multiple contributions as a team.	You think of ministry as an opportunity to get involved and make a difference in the lives of others.
4			You tend to select ministry partners, intentionally handpicking your team members..	You tend to involve anyone who's willing to serve.
5			You focus on developing others and delegating the ministry to them.	You focus on doing the ministry yourself, because then it gets done as you want it to.
6			You view ministry through "farsighted" lenses—looking to see what will be needed in the future, then building a team to implement the vision.	You view ministry through "nearsighted" lenses—looking to see what's needed now, then acting to accomplish it with the people on the team.
7			Your most "anointed moments" occur when equipping others to carry out God's purpose for their lives.	Your most "anointed moments" occur when you're able to meet a need in someone's life or in the ministry.
Total				

Now add up your selections to get an A total and a B total. Using your totals, find your score below.

	A	B	Then …
Equippers	7	0	**you're definitely an equipper.** Your focus and activities seem to be consistent with other equippers. *Develop your gifts and ministry opportunities in this area.*
	6	1	**you're definitely an equipper.** Your focus and activities seem to be consistent with other equippers. *Develop your gifts and ministry opportunities in this area.*
	5	2	**you're probably an equipper.** You demonstrated some repeated characteristics that you should explore and further pursue. It indicates some real potential in this area, and you should *seek additional input from leaders and from those you minister with.*
	4	3	**you're possibly an equipper.** There were some mild indications in your style and approach of the equipper. Be open to what God might do through your ministry involvements. *Find the kind of ministry positions that will enable you to develop your equipper tendencies for additional clarification and affirmation.*
Servers	3	4	**you're possibly a server.** There were some mild indications in your style and approach of the server. Be open to what God might do through your ministry involvements. *Find the kind of ministry positions that will enable you to develop your server tendencies for additional clarification and affirmation.*
	2	5	**you're probably a server.** You demonstrated some repeated characteristics that you should explore and further pursue. It indicates some real potential in this area, and you should *seek additional input from leaders and from those you minister with.*
	1	6	**you're definitely a server.** Your focus and activities seem to be consistent with other servers. *Develop your gifts and ministry opportunities in this area.*
	0	7	**you're definitely a server.** Your focus and activities seem to be consistent with other servers. *Develop your gifts and ministry opportunities in this area.*

You need to know if you're primarily an equipper or a server so you can pursue the appropriate kind of ministry role. Each role requires someone with the passion and spiritual gifts that could be summarized as primarily an equipper or a server.

2. For the sake of illustration and discussion, use your A and B scores above to identify

to what degree you're either an equipper or a server. Based on your score, circle the corresponding percentage on the chart below:

	A	B	Then …
Equippers	7	0	100% Equipper
	6	1	85% Equipper
	5	2	70% Equipper
	4	3	55% Equipper
Servers	3	4	55% Server
	2	5	70% Server
	1	6	85% Server
	0	7	100% Server

3. At this point you should have an idea about whether you're primarily an equipper or a server. Now it's time to compare that with an assessment of your current ministry position(s) or role(s), as indicated below.

a. Identify your current position(s) or role(s) in ministry service in the spaces indicated below.

b. For each of these responsibilities, decide what percentage of your ministry time and activities tend to fall into each category—equipping and serving. Write the percentages below. (There are no right or wrong responses here! Just use your best estimate.)

	Postition/Role	% Equipping	% Serving	Total
A				100%
B				100%
C				100%

c. Now compare these percentages with the answer you circled in question 2
above. Does there seem to be a close match? Check your answers:

Position/Role A: ___ *yes* ___ *no*

Position/Role B: ___ *yes* ___ *no*

Position/Role C: ___ *yes* ___ *no*

4. What do you feel the Spirit of God is saying to you right now about who you are,
the role(s) you're in, and any changes you may need to make? Pray. Listen. Write
your thoughts:

_____

_____

_____

_____

_____

 # DVD: Watch Session 2, Part 2   `9 minutes`

Jesus was both a server and equipper.

Jesus Serves

His serving was evidenced by the fact that people came from far and wide to see Him, hear
Him, touch Him, and be ministered to by Him. He met needs directly.

Jesus Equips

Most Bible scholars believe that the public ministry of Jesus was already a year old when He
called out and chose the twelve apostles (Luke 6:12–16; Mark 3:13–19). From this point on, His
mission and focus shifted from serving to equipping. Jesus didn't stop serving; He simply put
His primary time and energy into equipping the Twelve. He was making deposits into others.

For example, even when He fed the five thousand in Mark 6:33–44, He met the needs of hungry people as a means to teach (equip) His disciples some kingdom truths about God's provision and abundance. Jesus was equipping them through His ministry to the crowds.

So Jesus was *both* a server and an equipper. He elevates the value of both serving and equipping.

Do what God has called you to do based on how He has gifted you.

The Equipper's Paradigm

Jesus modeled for us the equipper's paradigm

Today, equipping leaders do the same

The Bible teaches that both equippers and servers have a unique contribution to make to the body of Christ and His mission in the world. Neither can fulfill their calling without the other.

The User's Paradigm

Some "leaders" who may seem, at first glance, to be the most productive are really no more than skilled "users." They're not equippers. They express a dark side of leadership because they use people to accomplish their own purposes.

Instead of following the equipper's paradigm as modeled by Jesus, users distort it:

Experiencing LeaderShift, chapter 10

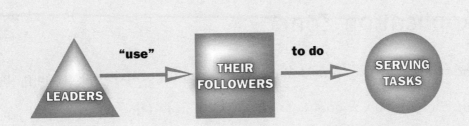

The real distinction between equippers and users is *motivation*, not style or giftedness. A user focuses on servers *for what the user can get.* An equipper focuses on servers *for what the equipper can give.*

Equippers and users will produce their own kind of fruit. One is godly; the other is not.

 ## Reflections

5 minutes

1. Do you tend to think of Jesus as more of a server or as an equipper? Why do you think that is?

_____

_____

_____

2. Jesus was equipping His disciples while ministering to the crowds. Is that kind of ministry approach possible for you? Why or why not?

_____

_____

_____

3. What do the equipper's paradigm and the user's paradigm say to you about how you're to work with people and tasks?

_____

_____

_____

Application Zone

The life and ministry of Jesus provides us the best example of serving and equipping.

Here are additional observations of what we learn from Him:

Jesus Focused on Serving

He met physical needs when He fed the hungry, gave sight to the blind, opened the ears of the deaf, and empowered the lame to walk. He even brought back to life some who had died.

He met emotional and mental needs when He cleansed the demonized, forgave the repentant, and loved the forsaken.

He met spiritual needs when He spoke truth that set free those who were in bondage.

His ultimate act of service was when He gave His life on the cross. He emphasized this aspect of His servant's role in Mark 10:45: "For even the Son of Man did not come to be served, but to serve, and to give His life a ransom for many."

Jesus provides us with the greatest possible example of servanthood.

Jesus Focused on Equipping

A broader look at Jesus' ministry reveals His life and ministry as primarily that of an equipper.

- As His ministry progressed, the amount of time He spent with the masses decreased, while He gave increasing attention to the few He was equipping. In the passages listed below, notice His focus on …

> *— the three* (Peter, James, and John): Mark 5:37; 13:3
>
> *— the twelve* (apostles): Luke 6:13; 9:10; 22:14
>
> *— the seventy:* Luke 10:1–24
>
> *— the 120:* Luke 24:46–53; Acts 1:8–15
>
> *— the masses:* Matthew 5:1ff.; 7:28—8:1; Luke 9:10–11

- Jesus focused on the *ministers* themselves as much as He did their ministry (Luke 10:17–24).

- Having seen Jesus pour His life completely into them, the disciples saw themselves as the end product of His ministry. They had a number of discussions about who would be the greatest in the kingdom, and who would sit where, all because they thought, "*We're it.*" (See Matt. 18:1–4; 20:20–26; Mark 9:33–35; Luke 22:24–27.)

- Not until the very end of Jesus' earthly ministry did the disciples become significantly aware of the larger task they were being assigned. He did not clarify this mission until His earthly life was nearly over. They were being equipped for the Great Commission (Matt. 28:18–20; Acts 1:8).

The reasons for His focus on equipping are easy to understand.

First, Jesus' earthly ministry was soon coming to an end, so He needed to train others to carry on once He was gone.

Second, although Jesus had come to reach the entire world, His ministry had been geographically limited. He needed to prepare others to carry His message to the "remotest part of the earth."

So Jesus was placing the future hope of His kingdom in the hands of a small group of people He had equipped—and who would continue to be empowered through the Holy Spirit.

Just before His ascension to heaven, Jesus instructed His small group of equipped followers to wait in Jerusalem for the power that had been promised them (Acts 1:4–8). It was this power that would enable them to be His witnesses in Jerusalem, Judea, Samaria, and even the remotest parts of the earth.

Characteristics of Equippers and Users

All of us from time to time have used people. Examine the following motivational characteristics of *equippers* and *users,* and compare them with your own.

Equippers	Users
Equippers relate to servers in order to *give* them something.	*Users* relate to servers in order to *get* something from them.
Equippers are able to create a loyal following.	*Users* cycle through servers.
Equippers cause those they lead to feel loved, valued, and appreciated for who they are.	*Users* cause those they lead to feel "used," sometimes to the point of being resentful. They feel they're valued as long as they make a valued contribution.
Equippers see servers (those they lead in the work of the ministry) as the focus of their personal ministry. They receive their greatest attention and energy.	*Users* see the ministry "program" as the focus of their ministry. The programs, events, and activities receive their greatest attention and energy.
Equippers see the servers they lead as an "end" result of their ministry.	*Users* see the servers they lead as a means to an end (the *end* being a program's success, usually defined by numerical growth).
Equippers see the ministry programs, events, and activities as vehicles to develop the servers they lead.	*Users* see the servers they lead as a vehicle to get the ministry programs, events, and activities carried out.
Equippers invest in those who serve under their leadership.	*Users* invest primarily in those servers who make the greatest contribution to the ministry.
Equippers derive their greatest satisfaction from the "success" of those they're leading.	*Users* derive their greatest satisfaction from the results being achieved in the ministry.
Equippers see people and their relationship with them as what is of value.	*Users* see people and their relationship with them as expendable, especially if they're not making a valued contribution to the ministry.
Equippers measure ministry success in terms of the process as well as the product. How we achieved the results is as important as the results themselves.	*Users* measure success in terms of the "end product" alone. They see ministry success in terms of nickels and noses.
Equippers very seldom need to use their position of authority to accomplish ministry objectives. Those they lead value their authenticity, vulnerability, and humility, and they trust their leader's heart for them and the ministry.	*Users* can be demanding and often resort to applying pressure to accomplish ministry objectives.

A couple of cautions:

- Users are sometimes soft-talkers. They can present themselves as relational and caring, but are really skillful manipulators. In the end, their manipulation is felt as "usery," and it's resented.

- Skilled users will tend (sometimes unintentionally) to build a user culture within the ministry.

How can you be aware of and avoid "usery" in your own ministry?

Avoiding "Usery"

1. After seeing the distinction between *equippers* and *users*, what are you feeling right now?

   _____

   _____

   _____

2. All of us have used people in one way or another. In what ways are you most likely or tempted to do this?

   _____

   _____

   _____

3. What practical steps can you take to move away from using people?

   _____

   _____

   _____

4. What biblical passages or principles come to mind that could help you to avoid using people? List them here.

_____

_____

_____

The Purpose of Equipping and Serving

In Ephesians 4:11–12, God tells us that equippers equip servers to serve.

But for what purpose? What happens when we obey this plan?

When we read on in this passage (in verses 13–16), we discover the answer. Here we find the purpose for verses 11–12—the reasons leaders are to be equipping servers to serve:

> Until we all attain to the unity of the faith, and of the knowledge of the Son of God, to a mature man, to the measure of the stature which belongs to the fullness of Christ. As a result, we are no longer to be children, tossed here and there by waves and carried about by every wind of doctrine, by the trickery of men, by craftiness in deceitful scheming; but speaking the truth in love, we are to grow up in all aspects into Him who is the head, even Christ, from whom the whole body, being fitted and held together by what every joint supplies, according to the proper working of each individual part, causes the growth of the body for the building up of itself in love.

Notice carefully the results indicated in this passage:

- We enjoy *unity* in the faith.

- We grow in our *knowledge of God.*

- We develop Christlike *character* in one another.

- We help develop in all a strong and stable *foundation* of faith.

- We speak the *truth* to one another in *love*.

- We *contribute* to one another's lives.

- We all *grow* into a *loving community*.

When equippers equip servers to serve, the body of Christ becomes a *unified, Christlike, strong, stable, truth-speaking, need-meeting, growing, loving community*.

Isn't that what we're all trying to attain in and through our ministries and the church?

Equippers equipping servers to serve will release more of God's presence and power to bring about the fruit of Ephesians 4:13–16. When verse-11 people equip verse-12 people to serve, everyone functions in the zone of God's anointing.

Prayer and Action

Take a moment and talk with your heavenly Father. Acknowledge His lordship over you, over the ministry team, and over the church. Ask how you can better participate with His plan to equip the members of your ministry team.

Write out whatever you hear from Him.

_____

_____

_____

_____

_____

Fork in the Road

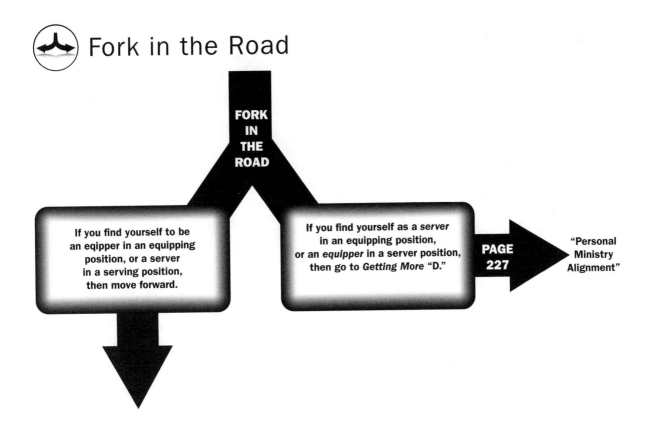

FORK IN THE ROAD

If you find yourself to be an eqipper in an equipping position, or a server in a serving position, then move forward.

If you find yourself as a *server* in an equipping position, or an *equipper* in a server position, then go to *Getting More* "D."

PAGE 227

"Personal Ministry Alignment"

 ## Next Steps

60 minutes

Now that you better understand the content of session 2, use these Next Steps to further your personal application.

It's time to get up close and personal about the people and positions in your ministry. The following exercise will help you understand these people more clearly, as well as the positions they fill. Most importantly, you'll examine whether each person and position are the right match.

Be sure to complete these Next Steps before moving on to session 3.

Ministry Team Alignment

In this exercise, you'll do these three things:

- List the names of your team members and indicate if each member is primarily a server or an equipper.

- Identify the position or role each member is in and indicate if it's primarily a serving position or an equipping position.

- Decide whether you have each equipper in an equipping position and each server in a serving position.

As you consider the primary equipping and serving roles of your people and the positions through which they serve, keep the following in mind:

- These identifications are *not* meant to be labels. Just as we identify people with different spiritual gifts, this distinction of "server" or "equipper" can also be clarifying and helpful—for them, for the entire ministry team, and for you as a leader.

- Some people may be involved in more than one ministry. In one, they might be functioning in an equipping position (small group leader, women's ministry director, etc.), while in your ministry they're in a serving position. Your goal here is to identify who they *primarily* are as *persons* (equippers or servers).

- Some people on your team may be developing as future equippers while functioning now primarily as servers. Pay attention to this as you nurture, develop, and coach them. Over time, a clearer picture of their calling will be revealed.

- If you don't know enough about some people to make a determination, spend time with them to talk and get to know them better. Walk them through the equipper/server differences you've learned about in this session. It would be helpful to have them complete the exercise in this session titled "Your Equipper-Server Quotient" (DVD downloadable).

- *An equipping person* is able to identify, attract, develop, and lead others so that they're using their spiritual gifts in a place of ministry passion to be faithful, fruitful, and fulfilled, thereby making God famous.

- *A serving person* ministers to people directly and personally, or completes a task successfully, thus fulfilling the ministry to which God has created and called him or her.

Directions

1. In the left column of the following chart, list the names of each person in your ministry. (Use another sheet of paper if necessary.)

   Next to each person's name …
   - circle E if that person is *primarily* an equipper.
   - circle S if that person is *primarily* a server.
   - circle ? if you're unsure.

(You'll fill out the remaining columns in just a moment.)

Name		Ministry Position/Role		Match?	
	E S ?		E S ?	Y N ?	
	E S ?		E S ?	Y N ?	
	E S ?		E S ?	Y N ?	
	E S ?		E S ?	Y N ?	
	E S ?		E S ?	Y N ?	
	E S ?		E S ?	Y N ?	
	E S ?		E S ?	Y N ?	
	E S ?		E S ?	Y N ?	
	E S ?		E S ?	Y N ?	
	E S ?		E S ?	Y N ?	
	E S ?		E S ?	Y N ?	
	E S ?		E S ?	Y N ?	
	E S ?		E S ?	Y N ?	
	E S ?		E S ?	Y N ?	
	E S ?		E S ?	Y N ?	
	E S ?		E S ?	Y N ?	
	E S ?		E S ?	Y N ?	
	E S ?		E S ?	Y N ?	
	E S ?		E S ?	Y N ?	
	E S ?		E S ?	Y N ?	

2. For all your "unsure" responses in that left column, identify here the reasons you're

unsure, and the actions you'll take to bring clarity.

Name	Reason	Action Step

3. Returning to the chart under question 1, list each person's position or role in the middle column. Next to each position title …

- circle E if that position is *primarily* one of equipping.

- circle S if that position is *primarily* one of serving.

- circle ? if you're unsure.

4. Again using the chart under question 1, observe whether your equippers are in equipping positions and your servers are in serving positions. In the right column …

- circle Y if you have an equipper in an equipping position or a server in a serving position.

- circle N if you have an equipper in a server position or a server in an equipper position.

- circle ? if you're unsure.

Ministry Matches

Now carefully consider what this exercise has revealed.

*For every **Y** response* on ministry match, give God thanks. Affirm the servant, and continue to equip him or her.

*For every **N** response,* consider the following:

- List here the person's name, the reason you put an N, and what actions steps you will need to take:

Name	Reason	Action Step

- When people aren't serving in the zone of God's anointing for them, they and everyone associated with them suffer the consequences of their being misplaced. Don't just pretend it's okay.

For every "unsure" response on ministry match, what action steps will you take in the next thirty days to bring clarity to who they are and how they're serving, so they too can be aligned in your ministry team according to the zone of God's anointing for them?

Name	Reason	Action Step

Part Two
THE EQUIPPING PROCESS

In part 1, we explored the plan God has for His church and the leadershift we need to make. We looked at the biblical foundations for equipping people and teams for ministry.

However, we've observed that many ministry leaders are taught and asked to function more as program planners and event coordinators than as the people-equippers God has called them to be (Eph. 4:11). Consequently, many leaders see volunteers simply as assistants to help them make programs and events successful.

Most of these leaders *want* to be equippers, but don't know how.

This leads us into part 2, which is all about the equipping process. Each of the next four sessions will focus on applying one of the four equipping phases:

Calling (session 3) is the process of attracting and selecting the right people for your team. It involves casting vision, and identifying and inviting the right people to your ministry team. Ministry success depends on how well you form your team.

Connecting (session 4) is the process by which an outsider becomes an insider. It involves a server's orientation to ministry, skill training, and belonging. This is where you help your members increase their competence and confidence and become teammates.

Coaching (session 5) is the process of putting more into your people than you take out. It involves investing, assessing, and expanding. This is the heart of equipping leadership and the means by which your people grow personally and as teammates.

Changing (session 6) is the process of leading change and managing transitions to fulfill the vision. It involves discernment, "carefrontation," and transition. It recognizes that people and ministries are constantly changing in ways that affect their life and ministry.

Session 3

CALLING

Perhaps the simplest definition for the word *leader* is this: "one who has followers." Without followers, you're not leading.

And to take it one step further, you can't be leading followers unless you're going somewhere. *A leader is someone who's going somewhere, with a group of people following.*

In this session you'll have the opportunity to clarify where you're going and to focus on getting the *right kind* of followers to go with you. Just like the attention given by professional sports teams to their annual draft of new players, or the time and care that cutting-edge companies devote to finding the right employees, ministry leaders need to focus intently on the makeup of their followers. *A ministry team's future success is largely dependent on who is selected for the team.* Equipping leaders understand this.

Unfortunately, when it comes to finding people to serve in ministry, the process too often goes something like this:

A notice is printed in the bulletin.

A verbal announcement is made from the platform.

A sign-up sheet is put out for those who are interested.

Then the leaders "take" whoever signs up—and do the best they can with who

they get.

Can you imagine this being the process for a professional athletic team selecting new players, or a corporation hiring new employees? Of course not.

Let's consider the way Jesus formed His team. In Mark 3:13–14 we read, "And He went up on the mountain and summoned those whom He Himself wanted, and they came to Him, and He appointed twelve, so that they would be with Him." Luke's telling of the same account goes like this: "It was at this time that He went off to the mountain to pray, and He spent the whole night in prayer to God. And when day came, He called His disciples to Him and chose twelve of them, whom He also named as apostles" (6:12–13).

While it's often believed that the twelve disciples became apostles when Jesus first called them to follow Him, this is simply not the case. Somewhere around twelve to eighteen months into His public ministry, Jesus went away for an extended time of prayer, as the above passages indicate. Following this night of prayer, "He called His disciples to Him and chose twelve of them." These twelve became apostles—His team. While we aren't told the specific content of Jesus' prayer that night, we can assume that a portion of it was devoted to asking His Father for the names of the Twelve.

Jesus carefully invested in *calling*. And just as He called certain of His followers to play a specific role in His ministry, we too need to extend a "call" to "some" to play a specific ministry role.

In this session we want to unfold the principles, perspectives, and practices for how equipping leaders *form* their teams. Calling is the first critical phase of the equipping process. It involves *vision, identification,* and *invitation.*

DVD: Watch Session 3, Part 1

8 minutes

How do you equip?

It's a basic, critical question.

There's no single way to do it—but there is an *equipping process* that can provide a framework for equipping individuals and teams of people.

The Equipping Process

- Phase 1: *Calling*—Vision / Identification / Invitation
- Phase 2: *Connecting*—Orientation / Training / Belonging
- Phase 3: *Coaching*—Investing / Assessing / Expanding
- Phase 4: *Changing*—Discernment / "Carefrontation" / Transition

When leaders focus on these four phases of ministry, they'll automatically find themselves equipping those they lead.

An effective equipping process means that leaders are equipping those in ministry to be successful—faithful, fruitful, and fulfilled to make God famous.

Your Ministry Positions

There are many different ministries—elders, ushers, the parking team, small group leaders, and teachers of children's classes, just to name a few. And each ministry includes various kinds of positions of service within it. These positions have varied requirements, including

- different time commitments
- different levels of spiritual maturity
- different levels of proven faithfulness

- different spiritual giftings

- different ministry passions

We need to *think developmentally!*

Can you identify the various levels of ministry positions in your ministry? What are the next-step positions … and the next … and the next? What positions require the highest levels of responsibility?

When your vision includes a framework for the ministry, you're ready to go to individuals and cast that vision for their being on the team. You'll have a specific role in mind for each one.

M-Categories (Ministry Categories)

M-Categories are the different levels of responsibility your positions reflect. Your ministry should have a full range of opportunities. You will find specifics in the Application Zone following the DVD.

 # Reflections

5 minutes

1. How could thinking about your ministry through the Equipping Process (calling, connecting, coaching, changing) help you as a leader?

   _____

   _____

   _____

2. What does it mean to *think developmentally?* How would you do this within your ministry?

   _____

   _____

   _____

3. "A team's future success is largely dependant on who is selected for the team."
Agree or disagree? Why?

_____

_____

_____

_____

 # Application Zone

20 minutes

Calling is the process of attracting and selecting the right people for the ministry. It involves vision, identification, and invitation.

I. Vision

Articulating a vision means capturing and communicating the essence of the ministry by articulating a picture of a desirable future, causing those with similar passions to be drawn to the ministry team.

It all starts with a vision—both a ministry vision and a personal vision.

A Ministry Vision

A vision is a description—a picture—of a desired future. It provides an answer to the question, "What will this ministry look like when the mission is being accomplished?"

Put another way, the vision is a destination. It's the place you intend to go as a result of fulfilling your mission.

For a biblical framework for this, let's look at Matthew 28:19–20, where Jesus states His mission for His disciples:

Go therefore and make disciples of all the nations, baptizing them in the name of the Father and the Son and the Holy Spirit, teaching them to observe all that I commanded you; and lo, I am with you always, even to the end of the age.

Had Jesus gone on to further articulate this vision, He could have stated what we read in Acts 2:42–47, where we find a description of what took place as a result of that mission being accomplished: A community of people was formed who "were continually devoting themselves to the apostles' teaching and to fellowship, to the breaking of bread [worship] and to prayer." As a result of such devotion, the power of God was on display among them: "Everyone kept feeling a sense of awe; and many wonders and signs were taking place" (v. 43). They were sharing all that they had with one another so that no one was left without (vv. 44–45). They were united in their commitment and met regularly together for fellowship (v. 46). And they worshipped the Lord together and received favor from those in the surrounding community in such a way that many were being added to their community (v. 47).

Had Jesus provided this description in advance, He would have been casting a vision.

We trust that you have a clear understanding of the mission of your ministry. (If not, we strongly encourage you to stop and do the necessary praying, thinking, and discussing to identify and articulate it.)

With your mission clearly identified and articulated, you now need to answer this question: "What will this ministry look like when the mission is being accomplished?" Write a description. Draw a picture using words. The clearer, the better; the more specific, the more beneficial.

While the people you're calling to join your team need to know the mission of the ministry, it's the vision that will really capture their imagination. The casting of a vision is at the heart of calling.

A Personal Vision

With the ministry vision clearly cast, every potential team member needs to know, "What role can I play in the fulfillment of this vision?" They want to know what contribution you believe God has equipped them to make toward the fulfillment of this vision. The answer becomes their *personal* vision.

The equipping leader is one who casts a personal vision to each potential teammate, so that each person clearly understands the role and significance of his or her contribution. Remember, you are *not* recruiting them to fulfill a responsibility; you're inviting them to embrace a calling to make a contributionin in fulfillment of a mission and a vision. This is where the equipping process begins.

Ministry Categories

Ministry teams that don't have a full range of developmental opportunities will experience constant turnover. People need appropriate levels of service to which they can commit. As their confidence, time, and competence increases, they'll be prepared to take on additional assignments. If that isn't available on your team, they may transition to another ministry.

Think developmentally!

As a ministry leader, keep in mind the whole of the ministry and how all the positions fit together and complement each other.

Remember too that people aren't static. They're forever changing as they keep developing their gifts and growing in Christ. Some on your team are just beginning to serve for the first time, while others are maturing and becoming equippers in their own areas of responsibility.

That's the purpose for ministry categories.

Familiarize yourself with the following two charts. They offer you a foundation for approaching your people developmentally. Later, you'll create Ministry Position Descriptions in each of these categories for your ministry.

Ministry Category	Faithfulness Factor	Time and Talent Factors
M1	Has a servant's heart and desires to take some first steps	• Minimum time availability required (1–2 hrs/wk) • Ministry passions and spiritual gifts are untested • Specific skills and experiences aren't required • Servant may not need to be a believer • Church membership isn't required
M2	Is pursuing a ministry fit that reflects his or her passion and gifts	• Moderate time availability required (2–4 hrs/wk) • Passion for ministry in general • A fit for spiritual gift and style may be required • Some specific skills and experiences are helpful • Servant must be a believer • Church membership isn't required
M3	Has developed ministry effectiveness with relational credibility	• Substantial time availability required (5–7 hrs/wk) • Passion for this specific ministry • A fit for spiritual gift and style • Specific skills and experiences needed • Servant must be a growing and stable believer • Church membership may be required
M4	Is performing major ministry responsibilities, equipping and overseeing people	• Significant time availability required (7+ hrs/wk) • Ministry passion proven and affirmed • A fit for spiritual gift and style • Proven skills and experiences may be required • Must be a mature believer, an example for others • Church membership required

Here are examples of each category from both the children's ministry and a small groups ministry:

Ministry Category	Example in Children's Ministry	Example in Small Groups Ministry
M1	Greeter, hospitality	Information booth assistant
M2	Discussion group facilitator	Hospitality team
M3	Lead teacher	Small group leader
M4	Elementary department coordinator	Coach of small group leaders

Identifying the appropriate ministry category for each position is important. Be sure your ministry has at least a few positions in each M Category.

Note: Don't confuse a person's individual level of spiritual maturity and commitment with the position in which he or she may be serving. For example, you may have an M4 *person* serving in an M1 *position*. This can happen because the person currently may not be able to commit to the time or responsibilities required for a higher level but wants to serve somewhere.

Creating a Ministry Position Description (MPD)

Now that you understand the categories, you want to be sure about where each position fits in your ministry team. You may need to create some new positions to round out the levels and ways in which people can participate.

A Ministry Position Description (MPD) is a tool for casting a personal vision that reflects an individual's contribution to the ministry.

Let's try one now. Use the form on the next two pages to work on an MPD. Think of one specific role in your ministry, and complete all the information requested on the form.

INSTRUCTIONS

(1) What is the name or title of the position? People should see it and basically know what it is about. Avoid acronyms and cute names that are not descriptive.

(2) This position is a part of what ministry team?

(3) If your church has departments, what department is this ministry in?

(4) Is this primarily an equipping position or a serving position?

> Equipping positions will primarily identify, attract, develop, and lead people and/or ministry teams.
> Serving positions will primarily meet a need, solve a problem, or serve a person directly.

(5) What is the M-category or ministry level of this position? M-categories are shorthand to describe the general minimum level of development and commitment required to complete this ministry position.

> M1 – SEEKER—available 1–2 hours/week, gifts/passion/style are untested/uncertain
>
> M2 – NEW/YOUNG believer—available 2–4 hours/week, gifts/passion/style need to generally fit the person and the position
>
> M3 – STABLE/GROWING believer—available 5–7 hours/week, gifts/passion/style need to specifically reflect the position
>
> M4 – LEADING/EQUIPPING believer—available 7+ hours/week, gifts/passion/style are proven/affirmed, able to lead and develop people

(6) What are the top three specific responsibilities of this position? Be as brief and clear as possible.

(7) Which spiritual gifts would best enable someone to fulfill the responsibilities and desired results of this position?

(8) What is the passion you want in the heart of a servant who is going to serve in this position?

(9) Which personal style(s), if any, would be preferable for someone to best relate and stay motivated in this position?

---

(1) Position Title _____

(2) Ministry Name _____

(3) Department _____

(4) Equipper—Server (Circle) **E — S**

(5) M-Category (Circle) **M1 M2 M3 M4**

(6) Responsibilities (List top three)

A. _____

_____

B. _____

_____

C. _____

_____

(7) Spiritual Gifts _____

_____

(8) Ministry Passion _____

_____

(9) Personal Style _____

_____

INSTRUCTIONS

(10) What would be the "minimum" spiritual maturity level required to meet the expectations of this position?

(11) Are there any specific talents or skills that might be helpful in order to effectively serve in this position?

(12) Availability—Using the key below, indicate on the chart to the right, the general times when these responsibilities can (or must) be accomplished by putting the letter in the appropriate time block.

> **KEY**
> **(O) = Optional—may serve at this time**
> **(R) = Required—must serve at this time**
> **(S) = Services—can serve before or after the worship service they attend**
> **(F) = Flexible—can serve any time, check box**

(13) What other commitments are necessary? (For example, team meetings, training events, social activities, etc.)

(14) What is the minimum length of time needed for someone to effectively serve in this position? (3 months, 6 months, 1 year, etc.)

(15) Where are all the places this ministry can be accomplished?

(16) Are there any special requirements or restrictions that a volunteer needs to know before being directed to this position?

(17) How many people do you need in this position? How many do you now have?

(18) Identify the staff person who is ultimately responsible for this ministry.

(19) Who is the leader/equipper of this ministry team?

(20) What are the best ways to contact and communicate with the ministry leader?

---

(10) Spiritual Maturity (Circle MINIMUM needed)
Seeker—New/Young—Stable/Growing—Leading/Equipping

(11) Special Talents / Skills / Abilities

_____

_____

(12) Availability   ☐ Flexible

	MON	TUES	WED	THURS	FRI	SAT	SUN
AM							
AFT							
PM							

(13) Regular Meetings and Commitments

_____
What?   *How Often?*

What?   *How Often?*

(14) Length of Commitment

_____

(15) Location
___Church ___Home ___Other _____

(16) Special Notes
___**Membership Required** ___**Other** _____

___**Must Audition**   ___**By Invitation Only**

(17) Total Needed _____ Now Have _____

(18) Staff Person _____

(19) Ministry Leader _____

(20) Contact Info Email _____

Mobile Phone (_____) _____ - _____

Work Phone (_____) _____ - _____ x (____)

Home Phone (_____) _____ - _____

At the end of this session (Next Steps), you'll have the opportunity to complete an MPD for each position in your ministry, as you think specifically and practically about each one.

(For additional copies of the MPD form, download the PDF file from the Downloads section on the DVD. It's best to print them out back-to-back.)

 # DVD: Watch Session 3, Part 2 8 minutes

Casting a Vision

You need to impart a personal vision so that people are signing up for a meaningful contribution, not just a job that needs doing.

Ask yourself, "What's the vision for this position? What is the specific contribution?"

Casting a vision is like casting a fishing net—not everyone who responds is exactly what you're looking for. You need a sorting process to find an appropriate fit.

Identifying a Team Fit

The more significant the role in ministry, the higher the expectations and the better the team fit needs to be.

A *team fit* means that the team member connects well with you the leader, with the position you're calling him or her to, and with the entire ministry team. A good fit involves all of these:

- *character*—demonstrated ability to manage one's life to the glory of God (personal integrity and emotional stability)

- *spiritual maturity* (Christlikeness)—an authentic walk with Christ that's exemplary to others

- *ministry fit* (competence)—the necessary spiritual gifts and ministry passion to bring God's presence and power to the ministry

- *team fit* (chemistry)—ability to fit well relationally with other team members and fulfill the relational demands of the position

While no one is perfect, and we all need further growth, you should have a fairly good understanding of the person you're considering inviting to be a part of the team.

The Invitation

1. When you hear the word *recruit*, what are the first few words that come to mind?

   _____

   _____

   _____

2. What are the first few words that come to you when you hear the word *invitation*?

   _____

   _____

   _____

Would you rather be *recruited* or *invited* to serve? The words you use have power.

Once your ministry vision has been communicated and the right people have been identified for a good team fit, you invite them to join the team.

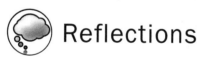 Reflections   5 minutes

1. Think back to the last three "invitations" you extended. Did you ask someone to simply fill a position, or did you cast a personal vision? How will you do it differently next time?

   _____

   _____

   _____

2. Does the principle of *sorting* and *selecting* people to get a good ministry fit seem too exclusive? What's wrong with just taking anyone who wants to serve?

_____

_____

_____

3. We suggested banishing the word *recruit,* and using *invite* instead. If words matter that much, what other words might need to be changed in your ministry vocabulary (*clergy, laity, volunteer, job,* etc.)?

_____

_____

_____

 # Application Zone   `15 minutes`

We looked at vision as a part of the calling phase. We are now going to talk about Identification and Invitation.

II. Identification

Identification includes interacting with and sorting the passions and spiritual gifts of those who have responded or may respond to the ministry vision. It means pursuing those who fit the Ministry Position Descriptions, or creating positions to fit the person.

Casting a vision is like casting a fisherman's net. *Where* we cast makes a difference. The apostle Peter had been fishing all night and caught nothing. Then Jesus told him to throw his nets on the other side of the boat. Suddenly Peter caught so many fish the nets were full (John 21:5–6).

Where you cast will likely determine the outcome.

People Pockets

You want to continually cast vision to the people God has been preparing to be part of your team. But you must be strategic and intentional. You must know what kind of people they are and where you're most likely to find them.

You can think of these people groups as "people pockets"—such as youth, new members, stay-at-home moms, men's ministry, or retired persons. You're pre-identifying the groups of people who are likely to have the kind of passions and gifts you're looking for.

You'll be able to call more of the right people to your ministry when you target the people pockets that are most receptive to your vision.

1. What is the vision God has given you for the ministry? How would you communicate it to someone in thirty seconds or less?

_____

_____

_____

2. Where are the people pockets most likely to respond to this vision? (Note the examples given above.) Identify at least six.

_____

_____

_____

3. Work out a schedule using the following chart for intentionally casting the vision to the groups you listed in the previous question. Plan to do this about every other month throughout the coming twelve months. What creative approach might be best for each specific group?

Month	Targeted "People Pocket"	Creative Approach
(Example:) October	Small groups	Invite small groups (talk to group leaders) to serve as ushers/greeters for a given month. Twelve groups would cover the year and give group members a common serving opportunity.

Also consider other "broad-casting" opportunities, such as ministry fairs, special events, and DVD testimonies. Strategically plan to cast your vision at some of these as well.

Here are a couple more thoughts to consider about identification in the calling phase:

- *Equipping leaders are selective.* They don't feel obligated to keep all those who respond. They know who they're looking for and stay focused on the right people having the passion and giftedness for building the team and expanding the ministry.

- *Equipping leaders are proactive.* They've identified what kinds of people are needed on the team and created Ministry Position Descriptions for each of them. If you don't know who you're looking for, how will you ever discover them?

Questions for Identifying a Team Fit

In the DVD, we talked about four factors that make for a good team fit: character, spiritual maturity, ministry fit, and team fit. But how do you determine if the person you've identified really fits?

We've prepared a list of questions in these four areas to assist you. You'll find them in section E, "Identifying a Team Fit," in the Getting More section at the back of this book. Take a minute to briefly review these questions. Select those that are most appropriate for the position and person being interviewed, or create your own questions.

III. Invitation

After vision-casting and identification comes *invitation*—asking individuals to join your ministry team, where they make the contribution God has equipped them to make.

We need to be very intentional about making an invitation. It should identify the position purpose with the individual's passion and gifting.

You're *not* recruiting volunteers. You're looking for followers of Christ who desire to be faithful, fruitful, and fulfilled in order to make God famous. When you invite someone to join your team, you're serving him or her. You're providing people with an opportunity to serve others in a way that makes God famous.

It's typical of many ministries to simply make a bulletin announcement, then wait and take whoever responds. But the equipping leader is intentionally casting a personal vision and issuing an invitation for someone to make a specific contribution.

When you extend the invitation, it should be done so that a vision is cast for an individual's role within the ministry showing how his or her contribution will make a difference.

Here are two examples of an invitation. How would you compare them? Which one strikes you as more appealing?

1. "I would love to have you help us pass out bulletins as people come to church. Just come fifteen minutes early and stand by that door. Welcome people and hand them a bulletin."

2. "You're a unique person—you have an ability to make people feel welcome and accepted. You have a warmth about you that puts people at ease almost immediately. I think God has given you the gift of encouragement [or hospitality, mercy, shepherding]. I'm wondering if you'd be willing to put this unique strength to work for our church. You can do so by serving as a greeter at the front door as people enter on Sunday mornings. You give a great first impression, and that's especially important for people who are new to our church. You would simply need to do what you do naturally and then help direct people to where they need to go next. You can also hand them a bulletin [or program] and perhaps point out the pertinent information on it for them. What do you say?"

One of these lacks vision, while the other has a compelling vision. Don't you agree?

We would encourage you to actually write out beforehand the ministry invitation you want to extend to someone. It needs to be personal, specific, compelling, and kingdom focused.

Think of a ministry role or position into which you would like to invite the right person. Write two or three sentences of what you would say to invite him or her to join your team:

_____

_____

_____

Ways to Sabotage the Calling Phase

We've looked at the positive and proactive aspects of the *calling* phase. But equipping leaders are also aware of the actions or inactions that can sabotage their best efforts. Be honest with yourself as you now consider this list of ways ministry leaders often sabotage the calling phase.

Answer each question; then write out a specific action step to avoid any sabotage in that particular area.

1. Do you have a clear vision for your ministry? (Circle your answer.)

   Yes / Somewhat / No

   Action step:

   _____

   _____

   _____

2. Do you have the ability to cast the vision? *Yes / Somewhat / No*

   Action step:

   _____

   _____

   _____

3. Do you intentionally *call* or passively wait for people to respond?

   Yes / Somewhat / No

   Action step:

   _____

   _____

   _____

4. Are you fully committed to gift-based, passion-driven ministry?

   Yes / Somewhat / No

   Action step:

   _____

   _____

   _____

5. Do you accurately assess the servant's ability, maturity, and commitment?

   Yes / Somewhat / No

   Action step:

   _____

   _____

   _____

6. Do you believe the myth that says "The wrong person is better than no person"?

   Yes / Somewhat / No

   Action step:

   _____

   _____

   _____

Prayer and Action

Take a moment to talk to the Lord. Acknowledge His lordship over you, over the ministry team, and over the church.

What has the Lord been impressing upon your heart to do about the *calling* aspect of the equipping process? What new insights do you have? What is He calling you to do?

Write out whatever you hear from Him.

_____

_____

_____

_____

_____

_____

 Fork in the Road

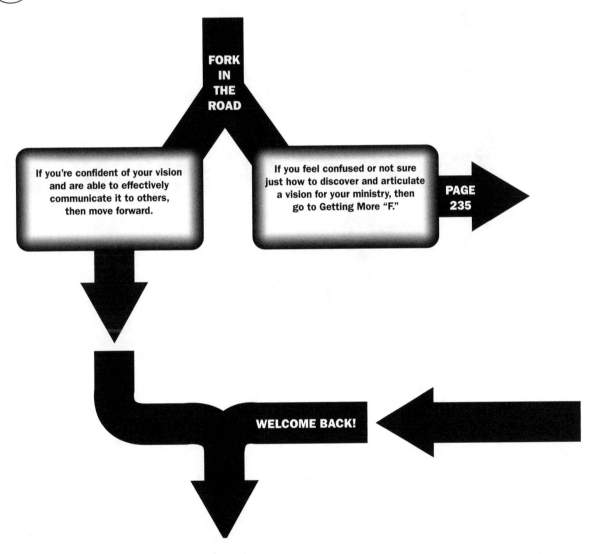

FORK IN THE ROAD

If you're confident of your vision and are able to effectively communicate it to others, then move forward.

If you feel confused or not sure just how to discover and articulate a vision for your ministry, then go to Getting More "F."

PAGE 235

WELCOME BACK!

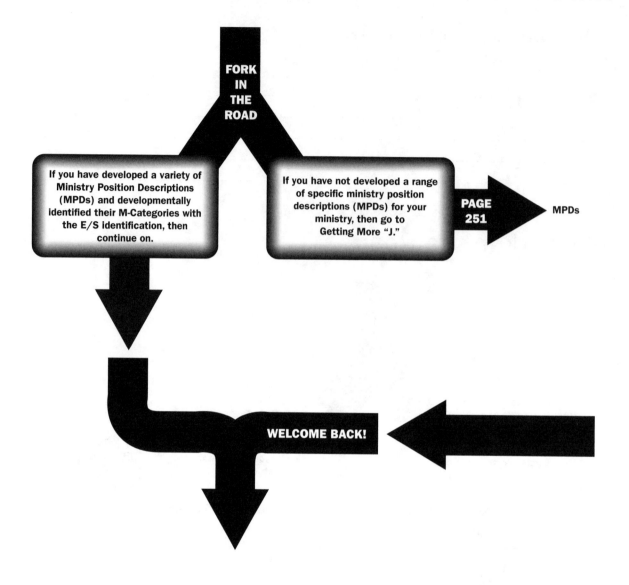

FORK IN THE ROAD

If you have developed a variety of Ministry Position Descriptions (MPDs) and developmentally identified their M-Categories with the E/S identification, then continue on.

If you have not developed a range of specific ministry position descriptions (MPDs) for your ministry, then go to Getting More "J."

PAGE 251   MPDs

WELCOME BACK!

 Next Steps   90 minutes

Now that you better understand the concept of *calling*, use these Next Steps to further its implementation in your ministry by …

- aligning your people and ministry.

- completing your Ministry Position Descriptions (MPDs).

Be sure to complete your Next Steps before moving on to session 4.

Aligning Your Ministry to the Church

How aligned is your ministry with the mission of your church?

Some ministry leaders feel frustrated and don't know why. They feel a lack of congruence within the team and wonder why there's a lack of fruitfulness. Besides the possibility of equippers and servers being mismatched (as we discussed earlier), their ministry may also lack synergy with other ministries and with the church as a whole.

Two things need to happen:

1. Team members must be in alignment with your ministry mission and vision.

2. Your ministry must be in alignment with the church's mission and vision.

Aligning a Ministry Team with Ministry Mission and Vision

Do the people and their gifts line up with your ministry's purpose and vision?

You need to understand your people and the gifts they bring, and to recognize when your people aren't functioning as a team. Be aware of which necessary gifts are missing, keeping the team from accomplishing ministry goals. It's futile to strive toward an unattainable goal if you don't have the right people. You need to either …

- redefine a reachable target for the team, or

- add the people to build the team you need for reaching the purpose you've defined.

Complete the following

1. What is the mission of your ministry? Why does it exist? (To see a sample list of answers, turn to section G, "Ministry Mission Statements," in the Getting More section at the back of this book.)

   _____

   _____

   _____

2. Which of the spiritual gifts are most needed to accomplish the mission of your ministry?

   _____

   _____

   _____

3. The following chart lists spiritual gifts identified in the New Testament. For each one, enter the names of people on your ministry team who manifest that gift. Remember, they can have more than one gift. When a gift represents that person's *top* spiritual gift, circle his or her name.

   ("S / E" in the chart refers to serving or equipping.)

Gift	S / E	Contribution	Names
Administration	S	Efficiency	
Apostleship	E	New ministries	
Craftsmanship	S	Hand skills	
Creative communication	S	Artistic expression	
Discernment	S	Clarity	

Encouragement	S	Affirmation	
Evangelism	E	Good news	
Faith	S	Confidence	
Giving	S	Resources	
Healing	S	Wholeness	
Helps	S	Support	
Hospitality	S	Acceptance	
Intercession	S	Protection	
Interpretation	S	Understanding	
Knowledge	S	Awareness	
Leadership	E-S	Direction	
Mercy	S	Care	
Miracles	S	God's power	
Prophecy	E	Conviction	
Shepherding	E	Nurture	
Teaching	E	Application	
Tongues	S	A message	
Wisdom	S	Guidance	
Other gifts			

4. Based on this overview, which gifts seem to be missing from your ministry team that would be needed to fulfill your ministry mission and vision?

_____

_____

_____

5. Are there any gifts you feel you might have too many of?

_____

_____

_____

6. Keeping in mind the vision and purpose for your ministry team, which of these responses is the most appropriate?

___We already have alignment and synergy in the way spiritual gifts are distributed among our team.

___We need to adjust the roles of some team members to create better alignment.

___We need to redefine our goals to reflect the gifted team members we already have.

Explain your answers, and list any action steps.

_____

_____

_____

Aligning Ministry Mission with Church Mission

Is your ministry in alignment with your church's overall mission?

Just as each spiritual gift makes a unique contribution to a ministry team, each ministry ought to contribute to the overall mission of the local church.

Complete the following:

1. What is the mission of your church?

_____

_____

_____

2. Briefly and clearly explain the role your ministry has in accomplishing that mission.

_____

_____

_____

3. What specific action steps need to be taken to better align your ministry with the church?

_____

_____

_____

Completing Your Ministry Position Descriptions (MPDs)

Go to the DVD, download the PDF file "Ministry Position Description Form," and print out the two pages back-to-back.

You should complete an MPD for each ministry position you have.

Then create your "dream team." Pray about the kind of positions (and people) you would like to have if you could find them.

Think functionally. Break your positions into reasonable responsibilities in all four M Categories.

We realize that some leaders themselves are not wired to do this kind of task as well as others, but it still needs to be done. If this isn't something you're comfortable doing, find someone with an administrative gift who can help you accomplish it.

(You can download over four hundred sample MPDs, which you can use or modify for your ministry and church. You'll find these at www.brucebugbee.com.)

CONNECTING

In the connecting phase of the equipping process, you're helping *outsiders* become *insiders*. To move people in this direction most effectively, you'll need to understand the difference between *group* participation and *team* membership.

In this session, you'll see how equipping leaders connect people to ministry in a meaningful way, helping them function as team members in the zone of God's anointing.

The way you lead will often determine a servant's loyalty and longevity to the ministry. How servants are introduced to the team and to their role and responsibilities will determine their true connectedness.

Consider two key questions every person asks when he or she starts a job in the workplace or joins a ministry team:

- Will I be liked and accepted? (Will I *belong?*)
- Will I be competent enough to make a valued contribution? (Will I be *valued?*)

The first question is about *security*; the second is about *significance*. Both represent deep-rooted needs all of us have. Equipping leaders give careful attention to these needs and the questions they prompt.

Your leadership influence will increase as you intentionally provide *orientation*, *training*, and *belonging* for the people on your team.

DVD: Watch Session 4, Part 1   `6 minutes`

Connecting is the process by which an *outsider* becomes an *insider*.

Connecting has three steps.

The first step is *orientation*:

> What does this new servant need to know about our ministry?

Step two is *training*:

> To demonstrate competency in his or her role, what does this person need to know and be able to do?

Step three is *belonging*:

> What will be required to help this new person feel accepted as a member of our team?

 # Reflections   `5 minutes`

1. What do *insiders* think and feel that *outsiders* don't? Make a list.

   _____

   _____

   _____

2. To what degree do you feel like an insider in the church or organization you're a part of? (Circle a number on the scale; 1 = I feel like an *outsider*; 10 = I feel like an *insider*.)

   1 2 3 4 5 6 7 8 9 10

   What causes you to feel as you do?

   _____

   _____

   _____

4. What kinds of things do you wish someone had told you when you started in your position? How would that knowledge have made a difference?

_____

_____

_____

 ## Application Zone | 20 minutes |

Connecting is the process by which an outsider becomes an insider. It involves orientation, training, and belonging.

I. Orientation

Moving from outsider to insider requires *orientation*. Remember back to your first days at a new job. One of the first things you experienced was an orientation process to help you become familiar with the organization. You were told all you needed to know to get off to a good start. Each person you add to your ministry team needs to experience this same level of orientation.

From Outsiders to Insiders

1. To what degree do you believe your team members feel like insiders? (Circle a number on the scale; 1 = they feel like *outsiders;* 10 = they feel like *insiders.*)

         1 2 3 4 5 6 7 8 9 10

2. What can be done to help them all feel like insiders?

_____

_____

_____

3. To help new team members become insiders, list three steps that could be taken by you or by someone you've equipped.

_____

_____

_____

Servants need to know *what* they're doing, *why* they're doing it, as well as the reasons for doing it the *way* they are. They need to know their way around. This means communicating how people, their position, and the ministry's mission serve together to meet the overall mission of the church.

This is where synergy starts. When servants understand how their particular contributions fit into the big picture, they find greater focus and motivation. They gain confidence that leadership is committed to overseeing all the pieces that make up the larger whole.

Leaders should be sure that someone visits with all the new team members to go over their Ministry Position Descriptions as a part of their orientation to the ministry team.

Note: This is another reason for having written Ministry Position Descriptions and keeping them current. Not only do these help you to know what you're looking for (calling), they also help a new team member know how to fulfill ministry team responsibilities (connecting).

Failing to provide a meaningful orientation creates confusion and uncertainty for the new team members, and will undermine competence and confidence—their sense of security and significance.

Ministry and Position Orientation

Remember, insiders know *what* they're doing and *why*, plus why they're doing it *the way* they're doing it.

Walk through the following questions thoughtfully.

1. What do new servants need to know about your ministry as they get started? (For example, the history of the ministry, how the ministry is structured, when team meetings take place, where to get needed supplies, and answers to the most commonly asked questions.)

   _____

   _____

   _____

2. Whom do new servants need to know in the ministry? (Such as other people doing what they will do, key leaders within the ministry, whom they report to, and key people in other related ministries.)

   _____

   _____

   _____

3. How does this person's role contribute to the mission and vision of this ministry?

   _____

   _____

   _____

4. What other information does this new person need to know? Make a comprehensive list of what should be included in the orientation process.

   _____

   _____

   _____

5. How will orientation be done?

_____

_____

_____

II. Training

Everyone wants to feel competent and confident in his or her role. This is true in all of life. The training people receive plays a critical role in their ability to make their contribution with competence and confidence.

Training has two dimensions:

1. _Knowledge_—What does this person need to know in order to make his or her contribution? What information must he or she assimilate and possess?

For example, before going into surgery, you'd like your doctor to know all about the procedure being done. As a fan of a particular football team, you'd like all of your team's players to know their playbook and individual assignments on each play. In the same way, every person seeking to make a contribution to the ministry needs to know certain information. This knowledge is provided through training.

2. _Skill_—What does this person need to be able to do? What skills are going to be needed?

Knowledge alone isn't enough; this person also needs to apply what he or she knows. For example, your doctor needs to possess the skills to perform the surgery. Your team's quarterback needs to possess the skill of throwing a football, and the receivers need the skill to catch it.

Everyone seeking to make a ministry contribution needs to possess certain skills. While some of these come easily and quickly, and others take much practice and development, there's always some skill involved.

The skills required for every role are initially identified and developed in training.

Complete the following chart by making a list of a few positions in your ministry, then answering the two questions below for each position.

Ministry Position	What do the people in this position need to know?	What skills do the people in this position need to demonstrate?

Training Methods

1. People can be trained in many ways. The possibilities include observation, role-playing, on-the-job training, reading a book, a "buddy system," to name a few. What other training methods can you can think of? List as many as you can.

_____

_____

_____

2. List here some of the positions in your ministry; then identify the best two methods to train someone for each.

Position	Training Method 1	Training Method 2

You should do this for *all* your ministry positions.

III. Belonging

In order for new servants to maximize their contributions, they also need to possess a strong sense of belonging as valued members of the team. New members should know whom they're accountable to and whom they should direct their questions to. They should also know *by name* all the people on their team—plus have access to their phone numbers and e-mail addresses.

Whether you use a buddy system, a mentor, or a coach, *someone* needs to be assigned personal responsibility for each new member.

Equipping leaders are concerned that those on their team are being ...

- spiritually nurtured

- personally cared for

- emotionally supported

- held accountable to make their contribution

How will you answer their question about belonging: "Will I be liked and accepted?" What will you do to ensure all your team members know they belong and are valued? List some specific actions.

_____

_____

_____

Being on a caring team tells a person, "You're now one of us."

 ## DVD: Watch Session 4, Part 2 5 minutes

We've been using the word *team* a lot. Now it's time to look more deeply at what we mean by *team*.

Over the course of your life, you've probably had many opportunities to participate with a group of people. Perhaps you belonged to a club, played a sport, sang in a choir, or joined the cast of a play. Maybe you've been in a Boy Scout or Girl Scout troop, a youth group at church, or a college fraternity. Plus you've probably held jobs where you had to work together with others.

When you stop to think about it, we do very little *all by ourselves*. Most of our activities and much of our life's work is done within the context of a group.

Considering all the groups you've been a part of, how many of those were really *teams?*

Feeling like you're part of a team is far different from just participating in a group. The very word *team* connotes belonging, camaraderie, commitment, unity, and purpose. If you've enjoyed a true team experience, the memory of it probably brings a smile to your face.

Mere group participation is okay in some cases. But in situations that really count, we want to play or work or serve on a *team*.

Group and Team Distinctives

A team is more than just a group of people working together. Notice the differences in the following chart.

Group Participation	Team Membership
Relationships are merely a function of a common involvement.	Relationships are desired and valued.
The *involvement* becomes a major part of your life.	The *relationships* become a major part of your life.
Individuals function independently.	Members function interdependently.
Individuals often compete with one another.	Members complement one another.
What *I* experience and accomplish is what matters.	What *we* experience and accomplish is what matters.
Individuals feel like a "lone ranger."	Members feel the team's support.
Individuals meet together primarily to discuss the work they're doing.	Members meet together to discuss more than the work they're doing.
Individuals focus primarily on the work at hand.	Members focus on one another and accomplishing the work.

Building a Team

The equipping leader is one who builds a team of people who do ministry with a deep sense of belonging, camaraderie, commitment, unity, and purpose. In the body of Christ, *team* counts.

It's your role as the leader to build an environment where team is experienced, and where relationships are developed and built beyond the work.

 Reflections

5 minutes

1. Describe your most positive *team* experience. What made it so?

_____

_____

_____

2. Describe a *group* participation experience. What made it so?

_____

_____

_____

3. Describe what your ministry would look like if it reflected a true team experience for all your members.

_____

_____

_____

Application Zone

`20 minutes`

You now have the opportunity to further assess your ministry team. Is it functioning more as a team or as a group? How will you bring leadership to your team and not sabotage this critical phase of connecting?

Ways to Build Teams

(DL)

Let's consider some powerful ways to build a *team*—which involves so much more than just bringing a group of people together.

Reflect on each of the following methods for building and strengthening teams. For each one, write down one or two ideas for how to practically implement it in your team.

1. Meaningful experiences together, outside your primary task …

_____

_____

_____

2. Praying together and for one another …

_____

_____

_____

3. Open sharing on a deeper level …

_____

_____

_____

4. Playing together—having fun …

_____

_____

_____

5. Encouraging one another—expressing affirmation …

_____

_____

_____

6. Dreaming together: *What might God do?* Brainstorming and strategizing together: *What might we do?* …

_____

_____

_____

7. Loving one another …

_____

_____

_____

8. Serving one another—meeting each other's needs …

_____

_____

_____

9. Celebrating together what God has done …

_____

_____

_____

10. Exalting God together in worship …

_____

_____

_____

Notice from this list that *team* is most effectively created when equipping leaders are providing experiences where team members are *together* and can be there for one another in a variety of ways.

11. What other ways can you identify that would build and strengthen your team?

_____

_____

_____

Teams and Groups

1. On a scale of 1 to 10, to what degree do you believe your ministry team functions as a true team, rather than just a group of individuals? (Circle a number on the scale. 1 = completely as individuals; 10 = fully as a team.) Rate your team, and explain your answer.

   1 2 3 4 5 6 7 8 9 10

_____

_____

_____

2. List a few actions steps you'll take in the next forty-five days to function more as a ministry *team*.

    _____

    _____

    _____

3. As you take the action steps listed above, what obstacles or challenges will you most likely face?

    _____

    _____

    _____

Ways to Sabotage the Connecting Phase

Leaders can sabotage the *connecting* process when they fail to be intentional.

The following is a list of some ways this can happen. Rate yourself in each area, and write out a specific action step you'll take to no longer sabotage your leadership efforts.

1. Do you make personal connections with members of your team? (Circle your answer.) *Yes / Somewhat / No*

   Action step:

   _____
   _____
   _____

2. Do you have an orientation process in place? *Yes / Somewhat / No*

   Action step:

   _____
   _____
   _____

3. Do you (or does someone you've equipped) walk with new team members through their first ministry experiences, helping them avoid feelings of abandonment? *Yes / Somewhat / No*

   Action step:

   _____
   _____
   _____

4. Do you impart a personal vision to each team member? *Yes / Somewhat / No*

   Action step:

   _____
   _____
   _____

5. Do you give each team member an understanding of his or her contribution and its value? *Yes / Somewhat / No*

Action step:

_____

_____

_____

6. Do you provide training so that team members feel competent and confident? *Yes / Somewhat / No*

Action step:

_____

_____

_____

7. Do you maintain a relationally connected ministry team? *Yes / Somewhat / No*

Action step:

_____

_____

_____

8. Do your members feel like insiders? *Yes / Somewhat / No*

Action step:

_____

_____

_____

Prayer and Action

You're probably having a number of thoughts and feelings right now. In the midst of them, the Holy Spirit wants to speak to you. *Experiencing LeaderShift* is encouraging you to experience Christ in your journey. Take this opportunity to reflect and listen to the One who is head of the church. Acknowledge once again His lordship over you, over your ministry team, and over the church.

What are you discerning about how you can increase your connecting effectiveness and better equip members of your team?

Record your thoughts.

_____

_____

_____

_____

_____

 Next Steps   `30 minutes`

Now that you better understand the *connecting* phase of equipping, use these Next Steps to further your personal application. Examine how your team functions and how it could function better.

Healthy Teams

Healthy and effective teams have four essential components:

- loving
- learning
- doing
- deciding

These four components are important foundations on which to create and build a healthy ministry team.

Each component needs to be present in every team for balance and development. If a team is focused only on *doing*, members might begin feeling used. If a team is committed only to *learning*, there might be a lack of accomplishment.

However, the percentages of each component will vary, depending on your team's purpose. For example, this chart takes four typical ministry teams and indicates how much time each one might spend in each of the four components:

Ministry Team	Loving	Learning	Doing	Deciding
Ushers	20%	15%	60%	5%
Church board	10%	15%	5%	70%
Discipleship leaders	20%	70%	5%	5%
Hospital visitation team	70%	15%	10%	5%

There are no right or wrong percentages for a given team. It all depends on what you as the ministry leader are called to do, and on what you see as the best way to accomplish it. But every team should be intentionally involved in all four—loving, learning, doing, and deciding.

Balanced Teams
(Loving, Learning, Doing, Deciding)

This exercise (adapted from *Prepare Your Church for the Future* by Carl F. George, and used here by permission) will help you to identify how your team is currently functioning, and to determine how you might want it to be balanced in the future. *(This would be a good exercise to do together with your entire team.)*

1. *Current Behavior*—As a whole, what portion of your time together as a team is *currently* spent in each of these four components? (Remember, there are no right or wrong configurations.)

   (Especially if you're completing this exercise together with your team, you may want to illustrate these percentages by drawing a simple pie chart. Do the same thing with the following questions.)

2. *Future Balance*—Now think about how you would like to see your ministry team function *in the future*. Carefully think this through, since some configurations might accomplish your team purposes better than others.

CURRENT MINISTRY

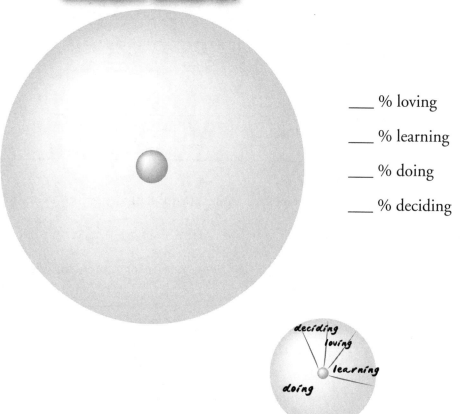

_____ % loving

_____ % learning

_____ % doing

_____ % deciding

FUTURE MINISTRY

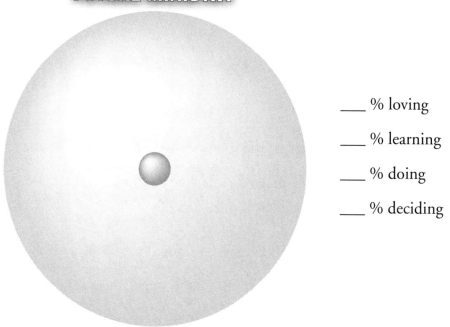

_____ % loving

_____ % learning

_____ % doing

_____ % deciding

As a whole, what portion of your time together as a team would you like to be spending in each of these four components in the future to better fulfill your team purpose?

3. *Strategic Steps*—What will it take to move from where you currently are to where you would like your ministry team to be? List a couple of action steps for each component.

Action steps for *loving:*

_____

_____

_____

_____

Action steps for *learning:*

_____

_____

_____

_____

Action steps for *doing:*

_____

_____

_____

_____

Action steps for *deciding:*

_____

_____

_____

_____

Session 5

COACHING

Imagine your favorite sports team operating without a coach. *Chaos* would perhaps be the best word to describe the result.

Or in the marketplace, imagine a sales team without a sales manager, a car repair shop with no service manager, or your local grocery store without a store manager. Whether the title is manager, leader, department head, or director, the function of such people in the working world is the same: to *coach* the players on the team.

That's also what an equipping leader is—a *coach*. Once a ministry team is called and connected, it needs to be coached.

So, what does a coach do? It's been well described in this definition: A coach is someone who helps you get where you want to go when you can't get there on your own.

Coaches wear many hats—instructor, mentor, disciplinarian, counselor, motivator, teacher, psychologist, protector, organizer, strategist, and cheerleader, to name a few.

Good coaches are hard to find. Great ones are few and far between. If you find one, you're blessed; if you *are* one, *you're* a blessing.

In the equipping process, the coaching phase is the process of *putting more into your people than you take out*. It involves *investing*, *assessing*, and *expanding*.

DVD: Watch Session 5, Part 1 `11 minutes`

We looked at *calling* your people through vision, identification, and invitation. We then talked about *connecting* them to your team through orientation, training, and belonging. We're now at the heart of the equipping process—*coaching*.

Every team needs a coach. A coach's role is to provide leadership, direction, guidance, support, feedback, and correction to raise the level of play of the players on his or her team.

After committing so much to calling and connecting your team members, how can you be sure to keep them long-term? By *putting more in than you take out*.

To "put in" includes building into them spiritually, strengthening their relationships with one another, having fun together, dreaming of a desired future as a team, enabling each of them to participate in a cause, developing their individual gifts and abilities, and providing meaningful affirmation and loving correction.

Personalize Leadership

A good coach knows the individual makeup of the people on the team and leads them according to their specific design.

Personalized leadership is meeting each person at his or her developmental level and leading that person accordingly. There are four stages that a person goes though in participation:

> *Crawlers* are the people who first connect with a ministry team. They need *direction*.
>
> *Walkers* believed they could make a difference; now they're not sure. They need *coaching*.
>
> *Joggers* have the skills and understanding to serve well. They need *support*.
>
> *Runners* have trust with high competence and high confidence. They need *delegation*.

Don't lead everyone the same way. "There is nothing so unfair as treating unequals equally" (Ken Blanchard).

Feedback

Let your team members know what you're seeing in them. Have the courage and humility to give meaningful feedback.

Feedback should be a part of your ministry culture. Create an environment that communicates your desire to bring out the best in your team.

The goal of this feedback is to create more fully devoted followers of Jesus Christ (faithful), more effective and difference-making servants (fruitful), and more purpose-filled people of God (fulfilled). It will include observations about their attitudes, performance, and relationships.

Coaches raise the level of play for each member of the team—putting more into them than they take out. Be that kind of coach!

 # Reflections   5 minutes

1. What difference would it make in your ministry if you consistently put more into your people than you asked from them? How might they feel? How might they serve?

   _____

   _____

   _____

2. Does the concept of *personalized leadership* for your team imply some inconsistency in how you treat everyone? Explain.

   _____

   _____

   _____

3. It has been said, "There's nothing so unfair as treating unequals equally." Agree or disagree? Explain.

_____

_____

_____

 Application Zone   `30 minutes`

I. Investing

The first step in the coaching phase is *investing*. Equipping leaders are investors. They consistently make deposits in those they lead. Just like your bank account, in order to make a withdrawal, you have to have made a deposit. You are investing in the lives of those you lead so that they have what they need to serve and make their contribution.

When leaders are putting more into their team members than they're taking out, people are nurtured and guided toward greater maturity. Blessing comes not only to the servant, but also to those the servant touches through his or her life and ministry.

Ways to "Put More In"

Here's a list of some tangible ways you can make an investment in the lives of your team members. These are some of the benefits a person should receive from being a member of your team.

As you go through this list, write down any ideas you have for how to achieve each one.

- *Spiritual life development.* Help them grow in their relationship with Christ. Their love and desire for the Lord, for His Word, and for abiding in Him should be ever increasing.

  _____
  _____
  _____

- *Affirming self-esteem.* Their contribution should result in a blessing not only for others, but also for them as they see the Lord using them to make a difference for His glory.

  _____
  _____
  _____

- *Personal care and shepherding.* Everyone wants to be cared for and nurtured, no matter how tough an individual may appear. To know that someone is watching out for him or her is a great gift that's always appreciated. This is what a shepherd does.

  _____
  _____
  _____

- *Spiritual gift development.* Great coaches take their players to a higher level of performance. Equipping leaders work to develop the giftedness of those they lead.

  _____
  _____
  _____

- *Skill training.* Making a contribution requires a skill, and sometimes several skills. A person's involvement in the ministry should result in the ongoing development of his or her skills.

  _____
  _____
  _____

- *Encouragement and affirmation.* Bring a word of blessing. Communicate in timely, specific, and personal ways how a person's presence and contribution to the team and ministry is a blessing.

  _____

  _____

  _____

- *Loving correction.* The people who really love us tell us not only what we want to hear, but also what we need to hear. This sometimes includes correction. When needed, the equipping leader brings a word of correction that says, "I love you enough to tell you what you need to hear for your ultimate benefit."

  _____

  _____

  _____

- *Purpose to life and ministry.* We all want to be a part of something bigger than ourselves, something that's making a difference. Give others that opportunity. Give them a vision of something more—something greater than life as it is currently.

  _____

  _____

  _____

- *A sense of belonging.* Everyone wants to belong somewhere—to feel, "I'm accepted here, I'm wanted here." What a blessing! The leader who's able to create a culture of belonging gives a great gift to those he or she leads.

  _____

  _____

  _____

- *A taste of fulfillment.* We all long for "soul satisfaction." We know that warm feeling within when God has used our life to bless another—to make a difference. A person's serving involvement should be an opportunity for consistent fulfillment.

_____

_____

_____

• *A sense of faithfulness.* Each of us wants to sense God saying, "Well done, good and faithful servant." Help your people sense God's pleasure with their service to the body of Christ.

_____

_____

_____

• *Fun.* Who doesn't like to have fun? And add a little laughter, one of life's great medicines. It heals, binds, melts, and molds.

_____

_____

_____

• *Worship.* Lead people to the throne of God so they sense His greatness. Help them capture the magnitude of God through times of praise and worship.

_____

_____

_____

As you look over the list above, consider the following:

1. Think back over the course of your life and recall the people who invested in you in a way that enabled you to experience the kinds of tangible benefits mentioned above. Write their names here.

_____

_____

_____

2. What other ways of investing in your team members can you add to the list above?

_____

_____

_____

3. Of all these various ways of putting into your team, which ones do you do most?

_____

_____

_____

4. Which ones do you need to emphasize more?

_____

_____

_____

Personalized Leadership

We briefly mentioned in the DVD the four developmental stages: crawlers, walkers, joggers, and runners. Let's look at them now in a little more detail, then identify the stage at which you see the members of your team.

The apostle Paul placed more value on connecting with people than on keeping to one particular approach or style. He was willing to be a Jew to the Jews and a Greek to the Greeks. In fact, he was willing to be all things to all people so that by all possible means he could save some (1 Cor. 9:19–23). He personalized his leadership, making himself and the message effective in the context of whatever his relationships and ministry required.

People are at different developmental levels. They need different kinds of leadership at different times. We're to "*admonish* the unruly, *encourage* the fainthearted, *help* the weak" (1 Thess. 5:14). That's personalized leadership.

Equippers think developmentally and practice personalized leadership. They understand what a person needs at a particular time. They also realize that the kind of leadership they offer at one point may be quite different from what they offer at another time.

Great coaches pursue what every team member needs, so that each person can be the best he or she can be—more faithful, more fruitful, and more fulfilled.

Your team members will be at one of four stages in their development: *crawlers, walkers, joggers,* and *runners.*

1. *Crawlers.* These are the people who are new to the ministry team. They may have had experience in another ministry, but they're new to your team. They tend to have a lot of energy and show great desire to make a difference. They may express confidence, but often lack the know-how that's needed. They lack the experience that true competence requires. Crawlers tend to be high in confidence, but low in competence.

   What crawlers need from an equipping leader is *direction*—"This is what I want you to do."

2. *Walkers.* After being a crawler for a while, servants then move into this second stage. They've gained some competence in their ministry position, but now their confidence may be shaken. The honeymoon is over, as they say. The reality of ministry has set in. At first they believed they could make a difference; now they're wondering if they really can. In this stage, they have increasing competence, but decreasing confidence.

What walkers need from an equipping leader is

coaching—"Let me help you with this."

3. *Joggers*. At this stage, they're experiencing a high degree of competence and variable confidence. They've got the skills and contextual understanding to serve well, though they still waver at times with uncertainty.

What joggers need from an equipping leader is

support—"You can do this."

4. **Runners.** This final stage is what the equipping leader is equipping the servant to be—a team member functioning with high competence and high confidence. There's a high degree of trust expressed through the willingness to delegate. This is what every equipping leader and servant wants to achieve.

What runners need from an equipping leader is

delegation— "I trust you to do what's needed."

Note: Delegation is *not* abdication. Abdication is a formal and clear relinquishing of responsibility and authority. Too many leaders think they're delegating when they're really abdicating!

So, the developmental level of each servant requires a different style of leadership from the equipper. Are you providing the right kind of leadership at the right time?

The following exercise will clarify how you can more effectively equip through personalized leadership. Put each of your team members into one of the four stages as you see them now. Identify one thing you could equip them to know or do that would help them move to the next level.

1. List here the names of all your "crawlers." Beside each name, tell what you can do to further equip that person.

Names	Action Step

2. Now list the names of all the "walkers." Beside each name, tell what you can do to further equip that person.

Names	Action Step

3. List the name of each "jogger." Beside each one, tell what you can do to further equip that person.

Names	Action Step

4. Finally, list the name of each "runner," and tell what you can do to further equip that person.

Names	Action Step

II. Assessing

After you've been investing in people for a while, you have to "hit the pause button" and assess the results. *Assessing* is the second step in the coaching phase. You need to observe servants and ministry teams and provide them with written and verbal feedback concerning their participation.

While written and formal assessments are valuable, it's often more significant to offer immediate feedback based on current observation. Consider some of the different ways you can provide positive feedback to a servant:

- a handwritten note containing specific and positive observations

- A one-on-one conversation following ministry participation.

- immediate and specific verbal feedback while you're ministering together

- periodic informal evaluations

- group feedback from the team about each one's contribution

- a formal evaluation process incorporating assessment tools

You want feedback to be a part of the ministry culture in order to bring out the best in one another.

Assessing is more than written assessments, although these do play a significant role. They can provide clarity for the team member and the leader. They provide a common language and framework for communicating feedback.

In this Application Guide, we've provided you with a number of written assessment tools to complement your observations, experiences, and the leading of the Holy Spirit for a clear and honest look at the role of team members and leaders. These assessments are included:

- Your Personal Success (session 1)

- Your Ministry Success (session 1)

- Your Equipper-Server Quotient (session 2)

- Assessing the Equipper's Ministry (later in this session)

- Assessing the Server's Ministry (also in this session)

We've also provided tools to assess your ministry structures (institutional and biblical), programs versus values, getting a team fit, ministry alignment, and other dimensions of ministry.

 # DVD: Watch Session 5, Part 2   7 minutes

God desires fruit. He intends that you and every member of your team bear fruit: "My father is glorified by this, that you bear much fruit" (John 15:8).

Expand Your Ministry

We want to be intentional about creating vehicles by which ministry can expand.

How will you expand the impact and effectiveness of your ministry? How will you grow the ministry so that it touches more lives? What can be done to increase the scope of your ministry so more people are served? How might you and your team bear more fruit?

Expanding your ministry will require a variety of strategies. We've identified and listed four key strategies—all of which are needed.

Strategy 1: Personal Growth

The initial way to expand your ministry is by increasing your own capacity for responsibility. The focus here is on your *personal growth and development*. For example, develop time management practices that enable you to accomplish more in less time; be selective about the people you spend time with and invest yourself in; be clear to identify priorities and address them with focus.

This is a good first step for ministry expansion. But you'll need to take another step because your personal capacity is limited.

Strategy 2: Addition

You can also expand your ministry by bringing another person alongside you, equipping that person to take on significant ministry responsibility. The focus here is *shared responsibility.* Two can do more than one. The work is divided between you and another person. In effect, you double yourself.

This, too, is a good step. However, it won't take long for the two of you to get maxed out. You'll need to move to strategy 3.

Strategy 3: Multiplication

An even better way to expand your ministry is to bring in a team of people who share the responsibilities of leadership. You equip a team of people who are capable of leading with you. Together, you "divide and conquer."

This is essentially what Jesus did with the twelve apostles and with the seventy disciples sent out to do ministry (Luke 10). He expanded His ministry by empowering others to do the needed work. Jesus sent out teams, multiplying His influence.

You need to follow this model from Jesus to expand your ministry. While this is a more effective way to expand your ministry than the first two strategies, there's still another, more significant strategy.

Strategy 4: Reproduction

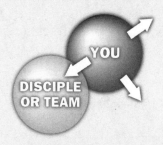

Reproduction is ultimately what equipping leaders strive to achieve. You expand the ministry by extending your leadership through a new leader. You're "passing the baton." That person then takes your responsibilities so you're free to move on and provide leadership to another ministry.

This reproduction process is reflected in Paul's words to Timothy: "The things which you have heard from me in the presence of many witnesses, entrust these to faithful men who will be able to teach others also" (2 Tim. 2:2). Reproduction is seen here through four generations—Paul, Timothy, "faithful men," and "others also." Paul played a key role in launching the church at Ephesus. He then equipped Timothy to assume leadership over the church, so Paul could move on to start other churches.

Reproduction is telling others you've invested in, "It's your turn to take over this ministry." Then you go and build into another ministry.

Reproduction is the ultimate strategy for expanding the ministry.

Each of these four strategies for expanding your ministry is good; all are necessary. While each builds on the principles and skills of the previous one, start with what's most natural for you, and grow into the others.

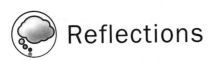 # Reflections

1. In your ministry, how have you distinguished between equipping *equippers* and equipping *servers*? Explain.

    _____

    _____

    _____

2. Which of the four stages of equipping do you do most, and why?

    _____

    _____

    _____

3. Which of the four stages of equipping do you do least, and why?

    _____

    _____

    _____

4. Do these four stages of ministry expansion excite you or overwhelm you? Explain.

    _____

    _____

    _____

Application Zone

How would you answer this fundamental leadership question: *What are you doing that others can do, while leaving undone what only you can do?*

_____

_____

III. Expanding

The coaching phase also includes *expanding*. An equipping leader discerns how to follow the Lord, increasing his or her Christlike influence through the growth of team members and the expansion of the team.

We've mostly been talking about how equippers equip servers to serve, which is at the heart of Ephesians 4:11–12. However, it's not just servers who need equipping. Equippers must be equipping other equippers, too!

While many of the principles and approaches are the same, there are some differences.

Equipping Equippers

Ultimately, ministry expansion is determined by a leader's ability to raise up additional leaders—equippers. The result will be that *equippers are equipped to equip servers to serve*. In this way, equippers find greater fulfillment as they see the work of ministry being accomplished by those they've poured themselves into.

Simply working harder and putting in more hours isn't going to get the job done. The job will be accomplished by equipping new equippers.

So, how can an equipper raise up other equippers to expand ministry? Here are some steps.

Step 1: Identify Equippers

The first step in raising up additional leaders is identifying those who are equippers by God's design. Here are some suggestions:

1. *Pray.* Ask the Lord to lead you to those who have the potential to be

equipping leaders in the future. This is what Jesus did when He chose the Twelve to be apostles (Mark 3:13–14; Luke 6:12–13). He went off for a night of prayer, after which He chose the Twelve to "be with Him." Ask the Lord to direct you to the kind of faithful people Paul referred to when he instructed Timothy to find "faithful men who will be able to teach others also" (2 Tim. 2:2).

2. *Observe.* Look for those who are leading others effectively. They may be doing so in another ministry or in another arena of life.

- Look in the *workplace.* Who is leading meaningfully and effectively in the marketplace or in connection with a club or group?

- Look for *giftedness.* We've already established the fact that there are at least five spiritual gifts for providing leadership for the body of Christ: apostleship, prophecy, evangelism, pastoring, and teaching. Look for people who possess one or more of these gifts.

- Look for *maturity.* Look for people who demonstrate strength of character as well as a spiritual hunger that will produce maturity in time.

3. *Discern.* When you've prayed and observed, you must discern whether they have the equipper characteristics we identified earlier. To help with this discernment, ask those you're considering to complete "Your Equipper-Server Quotient" in session 2.

Step 2: Equip Equippers

Once you identify those you believe have the potential to become equipping leaders, it's time to begin their equipping. You can do this by applying the very process you have been learning in this study.

Calling — Practice what you've learned in the calling phase. Begin by casting a vision of the contribution you want them to make as equippers in the ministry. Then invite them to embrace and fulfill this vision.

Connecting — Practice what you've learned in the connecting phase. Orient them to what they need to know about the ministry. Train them to demonstrate the skills they need to display. What knowledge do they need to possess? Group them in the relationships they need to be engaged in. Is there a team they need to form, build, and lead?

Coaching — Practice what you're learning in the coaching phase of the equipping process. What kind of leadership will they require? What sort of feedback will they need to receive? How often will you need to meet with them? In what ways do you need to "put into" them?

Using the equipping process as a foundation, your role is unique in equipping other equippers. You must share your responsibilities with them and challenge them to faithfulness and to reproducing themselves.

Faithfulness — Increase their contribution as they demonstrate faithfulness. Practice the biblical principle "faithful with little, faithful with much." Gradually add more to their role.

Reproduction — Challenge them to equip someone else, doing with another what you've done with them. You'll know they've truly become an equipping leader when they've equipped someone else to lead.

A biblical leader does as Jesus did and as the apostle Paul did, reproducing his or her life in others so the kingdom of God can expand for His glory and the good of others. Be an equipping leader.

Ways to Sabotage the Coaching Phase

Be aware of things you might be doing to hinder the coaching God wants you to provide.

The following is a list of ways ministry leaders often sabotage the coaching phase. Rate yourself in each; then write out a specific action step you'll take to keep from sabotaging your equipping efforts.

1. Do you repeatedly put more *in* than you take *out?* (Circle your answer.)

Yes / Somewhat / No

Action step:

_____

_____

_____

2. Do you provide regular and personal feedback? *Yes / Somewhat / No*

Action step:

_____

_____

_____

3. Do you provide personalized leadership? *Yes / Somewhat / No*

Action step:

_____

_____

_____

4. Do you equip equippers differently than servers? *Yes / Somewhat / No*

Action step:

_____

_____

_____

5. Do you develop ways to expand your ministry according to the four strategies? *Yes / Somewhat / No*

Action step:

_____

_____

_____

6. Do you provide assessments for your team members? *Yes / Somewhat / No*

Action step:

_____

_____

_____

Prayer and Action

Take a moment to talk to the head of the church. Acknowledge again His lordship over you, over the ministry team, and over the church.

Ask how you can increase your coaching effectiveness and better equip the members of

your team.

_____

_____

_____

_____

_____

 ## Next Steps

`75 minutes`

Now that you better understand the content of session 5, use these Next Steps to further your personal application. They include practical coaching resources in these areas:

- Who are you equipping to expand your ministry?

- appreciation

- equipper assessment

- server assessment

Be sure to complete these Next Steps before moving on to session 6.

 # Who are You Equipping to Expand Your Ministry?

The ways in which equipping leaders spend time with other equippers will be functionally different from how they spend time with servers.

Let's identify the equippers you're equipping and explore how you're developing them. Based on the four stages mentioned above, identify who you're intentionally involved with in each stage.

1. What specific things are you now doing for your own *personal growth?*

   _____

   _____

   _____

2. Who are you equipping for *addition,* and how?

   _____

   _____

   _____

3. Who are you equipping for *multiplication,* and how?

_____

_____

_____

4. Who are you equipping for *reproduction,* and how?

_____

_____

_____

5. Rank each of these stages 1 to 4 (1 = best) according to what you do best and are most comfortable doing.

____ Stage 1: Personal Growth

____ Stage 2: Addition

____ Stage 3: Multiplication

____ Stage 4: Reproduction

6. Identify action steps you'll take to improve your equipping effectiveness in each stage of expanding ministry.

Stage 1: Personal Growth

_____

_____

_____

Stage 2: Addition

_____

_____

_____

Stage 3: Multiplication

_____

_____

_____

Stage 4: Reproduction

_____

_____

_____

Appreciation

(DL)

We tend to have differences in how we most like to be shown appreciation. Are you aware of what these preferences are for those on your ministry team? How do they prefer to be appreciated?

1. Take a minute to look over this list of some common ways in which people like to be shown love and appreciation. On the blank lines, add to this list any additional ways that come to your mind.

   Then put a "1" and "2" next to the top two ways you like to be shown appreciation. (If you're married, underline your spouse's favorite ways. If you're not sure, ask.)

   ____ publicly expressed praise

   ____ a personal note

   ____ time off

   ____ money, bonus, raise

   ____ gifts, tokens

   ____ more responsibility

   ____ a recommendation

   _____

   _____

   _____

2. Now use the chart below to list the names of all the people in your ministry. Next to their names, identify each person's top two preferred ways of receiving appreciation. Not sure? Show them this list, and ask them: "If I wanted to affirm you or recognize you in some way for something you did, how would you most like me to show my appreciation? What's the best way for me to say thank you?"

Names	Preferred Appreciation Approaches	
	1.	2.

Equipper and Server Assessments

In the following pages, you'll find two personal self-assessment exercises for those involved in ministry. One is designed for those who are primarily in an *equipping* role; the other for those who are primarily in a *serving* role. Each has unique factors for helping you measure ministry success. They'll help you identify a path for personal and ministry growth.

(Additional copies of these can be found in the Downloads section on the DVD.)

If you're primarily an *equipper*, use "Assessing the Equipper's Ministry."

If you're primarily a *server*, use "Assessing the Server's Ministry."

Assessing the Equipper's Ministry

This self-assessment is designed for those who are ministering in an EQUIPPING role.

Directions

1. Complete this self-assessment.

2. Make a copy and give it to your leader.

3. Meet with your leader to discuss your self-assessment.

4. Together, come up with a plan for personal growth and ministry development.

Questions

1. What is the purpose of the ministry in which you serve?

    _____
    _____
    _____

2. What is your role and intended contribution in this ministry?

    _____
    _____
    _____

3. What do you spend the majority of your time doing?

    _____
    _____
    _____

4. What percentage of your time and energy is focused on equipping others?

    _____
    _____
    _____

5. What percentage of your time and energy is focused on accomplishing tasks?

_____
_____
_____

6. What specific skills, gifts, abilities, and competencies are required to make your intended contribution?

_____
_____
_____

7. Who are you equipping? (List individuals or groups.)

_____
_____
_____

8. In what ways are you working to equip others to serve successfully? (Be specific.)

_____
_____
_____

9. What aspects of your role do you enjoy most?

_____
_____
_____

10. List your major accomplishments over the past ministry year.

_____
_____
_____

11. What are the most significant challenges you currently face?

_____
_____
_____

12. What do you intend to accomplish in the coming year? (Your goals must be specific and measurable.)

_____

_____

_____

Summary

I believe I need to …

__ continue making the same contribution to this ministry.

__ make some adjustments to my role and contribution.

__ make significant changes in my ministry involvement.

Explain your answer.

_____

_____

_____

Personal Growth and Ministry Development

(To be completed *with your leader*)

A. Put together a plan for your personal growth.

This may include identifying or developing your spiritual gifts, learning new skills or time management tools, improving in certain character traits, focusing on certain spiritual disciplines, etc.

List here specific objectives and corresponding action steps for accomplishing this personal growth.

_____

_____

_____

B. Put together a plan for ministry development.

This may include pinpointing your next steps in the ministry's development, identifying key people you can equip to replace yourself, recognizing aspects of your ministry's strategy that need attention, determining how to manage future changes, etc.

List here specific objectives and corresponding action steps for accomplishing this ministry development.

_____

_____

_____

_____

_____

Assessing the Server's Ministry

This self-assessment is designed for those who are ministering primarily in a SERVING role.

Directions

1. Complete this self-assessment.

2. Make a copy and give it to your leader.

3. Meet with your leader to discuss your self-assessment.

4. Together, come up with a plan for personal growth and ministry development.

Questions

1. What is the purpose of the ministry in which you serve?

   _____

   _____

   _____

2. What is your role and intended contribution in the ministry?

   _____

   _____

   _____

3. What do you spend the majority of your time doing?

   _____

   _____

   _____

4. What percentage of your time and energy is focused on serving people directly?

   _____

   _____

   _____

5. How is your service to these people expressed?

_____

_____

_____

6. What percentage of your time and energy is focused on the accomplishment of tasks?

_____

_____

_____

7. What tasks are you engaged in?

_____

_____

_____

8. What are the most significant challenges of your position?

_____

_____

_____

9. What skills, gifts, abilities, competencies, and passions are needed to make your serving contribution?

_____

_____

_____

10. What do you find to be the most fulfilling part of your serving?

_____

_____

_____

11. Identify some of the major ways in which God has used your serving to meet needs over the past ministry year.

_____

_____

_____

12. What changes or improvements do you want to make in the coming year?

_____

_____

_____

13. In what ways could your leader better equip you to make an even greater serving contribution?

_____

_____

_____

14. What do you desire to accomplish in the coming ministry year?

_____

_____

_____

Summary

I believe I need to ...

___ continue making the same contribution to this ministry.

___ make some adjustments to my role and contribution.

___ make significant changes in my ministry involvement.

Explain your answer.

_____

_____

_____

Personal Growth and Ministry Development

(To be completed *with your leader*)

A. Put together a plan for your personal growth.

This may include identifying or developing your spiritual gifts, learning new skills or time management tools, improving in certain character traits, focusing on certain spiritual disciplines, etc.

List here specific objectives and corresponding action steps for accomplishing this personal growth.

_____

_____

_____

B. Put together a plan for ministry development.

This may include pinpointing your next steps in the ministry's development, identifying key people you can equip to replace yourself, recognizing aspects of your ministry's strategy that need attention, determining how to manage future changes, etc.

List here specific objectives and corresponding action steps for accomplishing this ministry development.

_____

_____

_____

_____

CHANGING

Ever tried to break a bad habit, or lose weight? Ever switched jobs? Moved? Had children?

If you've done any of these, you know that *change* can be a challenge.

Even when the change is positive and eagerly anticipated, it can still be difficult. As creatures of habit, we tend to be most comfortable when things stay the same. It's difficult to teach *any* dog new tricks—not just old dogs—because new tricks involve change. Change is unnatural, in that we've already chosen what tends to be most natural.

As a result, change can be stressful. Perhaps this explains why we tend to make changes so slowly and carefully, and only when really needed or desired.

This is especially true on an organizational level. Most of us have our hands full trying to manage our own personal transitions; add a significant number of people into the process, and it becomes clear that managing organizational change is one of the greatest challenges facing any leader.

How do I get others to see the need for change? What do I do with those who resist? How do I implement needed changes? How rapidly should change occur? What about the pain some will feel as a result of the changes we're making? How much change is too much? What if the resistance is really strong? What percentage of people need to agree with the change? These questions, and many more like them, face every leader who's trying to bring about organizational change.

You can't avoid change in your ministry or in the people who serve with you. The needs of the ministry will evolve over time. And occasions will arise when a team member feels called to a different position or ministry. Eventually you'll need to lead some of your team members through *personal* transitions. If you lead your ministry long enough, you'll also need to manage some *organizational* changes. In this session, we'll look at both of these.

Change happens both internally and externally. Personal changes are internal transitions—they're what happen inside us as we come to terms with external change. They usually take more time. How we navigate these shifts is important. Too often, leaders seek to implement organizational change without knowing how to manage the longer process of personal transitions involving perspectives, feelings, and attitudes.

The process of leading change and managing transitions to fulfill vision includes discernment, "carefrontation," and transition.

 # DVD: Watch Session 6, Part 1   9 minutes

In part 1 of this session, we'll focus on *personal transitions*. In part 2, we'll look at *organizational change*.

Personal Transitions

People often need help negotiating what is happening both within them (internally) and around them (externally).

While several factors can bring about such transitions, we want to focus on one of the primary reasons often overlooked. It's when a servant is "failing" in his or her current ministry role.

When a Team Member Fails

We've defined *success* biblically as being faithful, bearing fruit, and experiencing fulfillment in ways that make God famous. So, we can evaluate a team member as *failing* when he or she is not being faithful, bearing fruit, or experiencing fulfillment in his or her current role.

In light of those definitions, when someone on the team is *not* succeeding, change is necessary.

Common Reasons for Failing

Most often, people in ministry tend to fail for one of these three reasons:

1. *Misslotted.* They're in the wrong position. They're in a role that doesn't represent the zone of God's anointing for them.

2. *They're inadequately trained or led.* They're probably in the right slot, but haven't received the proper training. They lack the confidence and competence that comes from proper knowledge and skills.

3. *They're disqualified* (1 Cor. 9:27). They have a disqualifying issue related to their spiritual life, character, attitudes, or behavior. It could involve such things as a pattern of sin or unreconciled relationships.

How you approach this person depends on which of these reasons is contributing to his or her "failure."

It's important to note that the first two reasons for someone's failure point back to the leader. When a leader fails to properly place, train, and lead the servant, the servant often fails to succeed. *Speed of the leader, speed of the team.*

The third reason is a *servant* issue. When the character or attitude of a team member diminishes to an unacceptable level because of spiritual or relational brokenness, that person needs to step away from ministry for a time of healing and restoration.

"Carefronting"

"*Care*fronting" (rather than *con*fronting) means going to a team member to openly address reasons for his or her lack of success. Doing this is difficult but necessary.

When equipping leaders do this, they graciously speak the truth in love—something God has wisely commanded us to do (Eph. 4:15). As someone has observed, "Truth without love is brutality; love without truth is sentimentality." Christ, the head of the church, requires both truth and love from His equipping leaders.

Although these "carefronting" conversations can be difficult, we cannot allow people to continue in a ministry role where they're not being faithful, bearing fruit, and experiencing fulfillment.

These conversations will mean the leader goes in prayer, gentleness, love, humility, and grace to talk about the quality and effectiveness of the team member's ministry effort or success. The leader helps the team member recognize the reason for his or her "failure." Together they seek to understand how to better equip the person for a more God-honoring ministry impact. Necessary guidance is offered. If more training is needed, the leader steps in to provide it.

Leaders must also own their part for a servant's failure. What might you have done or not done that contributed to the situation?

The truth may hurt, but eventually, the truth will defend itself in a person's life. God will always honor the truth. "You will know the truth, and the truth will make you free" (John 8:32).

 # Reflections

`5 minutes`

1. "When a servant fails, most of the time it's a leadership issue." Agree or disagree? Why?

   _____

   _____

   _____

2. If a team member isn't being successful (faithful, fruitful, and fulfilled), what prevents you from talking to him or her about it?

_____

_____

_____

3. If a servant is misplaced in his or her serving, what's the difference between a *con*fronting response and a "*care*fronting" response? How do they *feel* different?

_____

_____

_____

✏️ Application Zone   `20 minutes`

Personal Transitions

Personal transition involves *discernment, carefrontation,* and *transition.*

I. Discernment

Discernment means making a careful assessment about what's happening in a team member's life and ministry and the reasons why. Through prayer, personal observation, interaction, and any appropriate assessments, you can discern what needs to occur.

Unsuccessful Servants

Take an inventory of all the people on your ministry team. Seek to identify anyone on your team who isn't experiencing ministry success. Do this prayerfully, and be honest with yourself and with the Lord. Don't pretend you don't know what you know.

1. Using the following chart, list the names of any team members you feel aren't currently experiencing success according to our definition of it—being faithful, being fruitful, being fulfilled, and making God famous.

2. Based on the three primary reasons servants fail in ministry, identify the reason(s) for each servant's failure (1 = wrong position; 2 = inadequately trained or led; 3 = disqualified; 4 = not sure). Put the number in the chart beside each person's name.

3. Identify a specific action step you'll take to assist each person toward a successful experience.

Name	Reason (1, 2, 3, or 4)	Action Step

Drawing from your identification of any unsuccessful servants, consider some options you can take to help them.

1. *Reassess.* With all your team members, review their most affirmed spiritual gifts and their greatest ministry passions.

Passion—Understand what God has put into these people's hearts. What is it they feel motivated to do? What are they most deeply called to? In what area would they most like to make a difference?

Gifts—The next step is to assess or reassess their spiritual gifts. Review the results of this assessment with them and discuss to what degree their gifts are currently being utilized in their ministry role.

(Resources to identify passion and gifts include *What You Do Best in the Body of Christ, Discover Your Spiritual Gifts,* and the *Network* course.)

2. *Relook.* Explore other ministry options based on the results of your reassessment. Those options may lie within your current ministry or they might be in another ministry altogether. Identify suitable options for their future that would most effectively utilize their gifts and passions so they can serve in the zone of God's anointing.

3. *Restructure.* Adjust the person's role or responsibilities within your ministry. This kind of tweaking is needed at times to keep up with personal growth or the growth or decline of the ministry, and the changes associated with that.

4. *Reassign.* Connect the servant to another ministry team so his or her gifts and passion can be more accurately expressed. Assist that person in connecting with a ministry that reflects God's zone of anointing.

5. *Recess.* Sometimes it's appropriate to take a serving sabbatical. This should be a time of reflection, renewal, and perhaps life-change. It's a passing season, not a permanent position. They stay connected with equipping leaders who will move them once again into the blessings of servanthood at the appropriate time. No one should be forgotten or neglected during a serving sabbatical. (You may want to create a ministry team that serves those who are not currently serving.)

What other options exist? List some here.

6. _____

_____

_____

7. _____

_____

_____

8. _____

_____

_____

Whenever a transition in service needs to be made, follow these proven steps to serve and honor the team member as well as strengthen the ministry. Equipping leaders should fully assist team members in this transition.

You've effectively transitioned a servant when that person becomes an insider on another team (called and connected).

II. "Carefrontation"

When you've put together your personal observations with any servant interactions and assessments, and you've considered the options, you should pray. After a time of discernment, it often leads to the need for *"carefrontation."*

Carefrontation means speaking the truth in love about the causes contributing to someone's need for a personal transition. It allows the person to grow from his or her experiences and continue in the zone of God's anointing.

Use the following practical insights with wisdom to help you in these intentional conversations:

- Invite several intercessors to pray for the servant, for you, for the issues involved, and for God's truth to be spoken with love and grace.

- Never have these conversations one-on-one—always include a third person. This could be another leader from your ministry or a staff person. It should not be one of the individual's peers.

- From the three reasons we've identified (wrong position, inadequate training, or being disqualified), indicate the one which is the most applicable to the person.

- Provide specific examples to support your thinking. If there's a pattern, show repeated behaviors. Make it clear. Connect the dots.

- Seek *understanding* first. Then, if possible, agreement.

- After the conversation, summarize in writing the specific issues and concerns you brought to the person, the relevant action points that were discussed, and what was agreed to.

- Go in prayer, with gentleness, a pure heart, and a spirit of love.

Remember, carefrontation is more about assisting people to operate in the zone of God's anointing than about focusing on reasons for their lack of success.

III. Transition

After you've applied *discernment* and *carefrontation,* you must now lead that person to make the necessary *transition.*

Transition means lifting up the value of servanthood by guiding and supporting a servant through the process of personal change, with the goal of leading that person to a fuller expression of the zone of God's anointing in his or her life

This transition will affect not only the individual, but also the other members of the team, and you as well. So before you actually make any changes, think through the broader implications of the changes being considered.

Personal Transitions—Questions to Consider

Here are some critical questions to ask and monitor as you lead a person through change.

1. For the transitions you're seeking to make, what are the implications for the servant, the team, and you—both good and bad, real and perceived?

For example,

- Will this person's position or role in the ministry change?
- Will the ministry be structured and organized differently?
- Will the changes affect anything in the way the ministry functions, or will any activities be redirected toward different goals, or even done away with completely?
- Are there any additional time or financial implications?
- Will certain people be asked to do more (or less) than they were doing previously?
- Who will be the primary person to assist this servant in the change process?

_____

_____

_____

Some transitions are clearly good; others will be seen as bad. Some of the implications are real; others are only perceived. Either way, they need to be identified so you can anticipate the reactions of those who are affected and work in ways that demonstrate care and concern.

2. Who else will be affected?

List the names of those who will be most affected by the implications you just identified. This is especially important for those whom the change will negatively affect (either real or perceived).

_____

_____

3. How will they be affected?

What are the specific effects of the transition? What will actually change?

_____

_____

_____

If the desired transition is truly from the Lord, and you're intentionally and skillfully walking with people through their transitions, you'll not only be successful, but also be equipping your followers in the process. The goal is to benefit your followers. This is at the heart of being an equipping leader.

Organizational Change

In the first part of this session we looked at personal transitions. This now completes the equipping process. Everything we've talked about up to this point was to help you understand biblically the basis for gift-based, passion-driven ministry through God's design of equippers and servers.

In this final segment, we will focus on your role in leading and managing the organizational changes that often occur as a result of implementing the equipping process. As you keep moving toward fulfilling your ministry mission and vision, organizational changes will likely need to occur.

DVD: Watch Session 6, Part 2   `10 minutes`

Organizational Change Dynamics

1	**Current Discontent**	When there's sufficient discontent with where things stand now, *there's motivation for change.*
2	**Future Vision**	When there's a clear picture of a desired future attached to the discontent, *there's motivation for change.*
3	**Strategic Plan**	When the steps toward this desired future are clear and achievable, *there's motivation for change.*
4	**Active Resistance**	When these three driving forces combined are greater than the active resistance to them—*change can occur!*

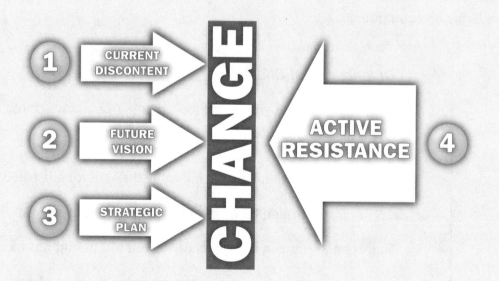

Implementing the Change Process

Implementing organizational change requires embracing four essential steps.

Step 1: Pray Fervently

The Spirit of God needs to go before you. Prayer brings the Spirit of God. Get people together to pray for the Spirit to be released (1 John 5:14; John 15:7).

Step 2: Teach the Word

Teach the Word to create understanding. People need to see that it's not you, but God, who wants the change. If you cannot justify the change you want to bring about based on something in the Word—be really careful.

Step 3: Lead by Example

Lead by example in order to provide illustration. You want people to see what this change looks like.

The combination of the power of the Holy Spirit, the truth of God's Word, and a living example of God at work serve to create a desire in other believers to experience God at work through them.

Step 4: Create a Vehicle

Create a vehicle to assist application. You may have owned the biblical value of equippers and servers for years, but haven't implemented it well because you simply lacked a vehicle to assist you in its application. That's why we created this Application Guide. It's your vehicle for experiencing a leadershift.

Experiencing LeaderShift <u>Together</u>

We've also created another vehicle to assist you in taking these critical biblical truths to your ministry team. It's called *Experiencing LeaderShift Together*. Having a common understanding as well as a common language is essential for organizational effectiveness. *Experiencing*

Ⓡ

Experiencing LeaderShift, chapter 7

LeaderShift Together will assist you in doing just that.

Paul writes to Timothy, "But you, be sober in all things, endure hardship, do the work of an evangelist, fulfill your ministry" (2 Tim. 4:5).

 ## Reflections

5 minutes

1. How do the organizational change dynamics help you in understanding how to make needed changes in your ministry?

   _____
   _____
   _____

2. Do the discussion on change dynamics and the steps for embracing change seem too mechanical to you? Why or why not?

   _____
   _____
   _____

3. To truly embrace the change process, what must you work on the most? Check one.

   __ praying fervently

   __ teaching the Word

   __ leading by example

   __ creating a vehicle

   Why? What will you do?

   _____
   _____
   _____

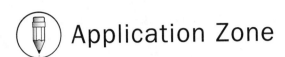 Application Zone

45 minutes

> ### *Organizational Changes*
>
> Leading through organizational change means assisting team members in making the changes required to fulfill the ministry mission and vision.
>
> The purpose of this Application Guide has been essentially to assist you in implementing gift-based, passion-driven ministry. Doing gift-based, passion-driven ministry is not optional—it's biblical. However, many ministries haven't embraced this conviction. We've identified some common fears associated with taking this biblical position.

Leading the Change Process

The following exercise is designed to help you gain a better understanding of your ministry's readiness for change. You'll also find it valuable as you're in the midst of a change process. It will help ensure that important issues are being appropriately monitored and implemented along the way. Often the trajectory of desired changes can get off course if you're not managing the process.

Current Discontent

Current discontent isn't just being dissatisfied. The Holy Spirit drives healthy discontent. It's God-initiated. If this is not the case, motivation for change will be lacking. It's essential that we seek God, to see if He is "discontent."

The greater the discontent, the greater the motivation for change. A little discontent will only bring about a little change.

Both the leader and the team must share the discontent. If one is discontent but the other isn't, change won't be possible.

1. What are the current realities within your ministry that you would like to see changed? (Some examples: "Some people aren't in the right positions"; "I don't have a gift-based, passion-driven ministry team"; "We don't operate as a team.")

    _____

    _____

    _____

2. On a scale of 1 to 10, to what degree is your ministry team experiencing discontent with the current realities you listed? (1 = no discontent at all; 10 = extreme discontent)

    1   2   3   4   5   6   7   8   9   10

    _____

    _____

    _____

3. In what ways are you experiencing the negative effects of the current realities you want to see changed?

    _____

    _____

    _____

4. In what areas would you like to see your team members experiencing a greater discontent? (For example, level of fruitfulness, degree of fulfillment, number of conversions, or tasks being done in the zone of God's anointing.)

    _____

    _____

    _____

5. In what ways could you increase the current level of appropriate discontent in your ministry?

_____

_____

_____

Future Vision

A vision of the future by itself isn't sufficient to create the change desired. Too many leaders are casting a vision that's unconnected with current discontent. A vision must meet the felt needs (discontent) if it's going to be a motivator for change.

A vision by itself isn't the answer. However, when an appropriate vision is clearly articulated and focused as a solution to the team's current discontent, you have a powerful combination that motivates people to move from where they are to that picture of a desired future.

1. What will the current realities be if the change you desire actually occurs? (For example, "Everyone is in the right position"; "My team is a gift-based, passion-driven ministry"; "We function as a team.")

_____

_____

_____

2. On a scale of 1 to 10, rate the clarity of your vision for your ministry (1 = it's fuzzy and confusing; 10 = it's crystal-clear and articulate). Explain your answer.

1   2   3   4   5   6   7   8   9   10

_____

_____

_____

3. On a scale of 1 to 10, to what degree do you communicate or cast a future vision for your ministry? (1 = I never cast the vision; 10 = I'm constantly casting the vision) Explain your answer.

1   2   3   4   5   6   7   8   9   10

_____

_____

_____

4. How does your vision address any current discontent in your ministry?

_____

_____

_____

5. How could casting a vision help generate discontent?

_____

_____

_____

Strategy

Strategy is a plan for how you intend to accomplish the mission and fulfill the vision. It's not enough to just have a vision connected to current discontent if the action steps needed aren't *simple* and *doable*. They need to be baby steps, essentially.

A vision without strategy leads to frustration. But *with* strategic steps, a vision will create movement away from discontent and toward satisfaction. When people can see how the vision could become reality, they'll have greater confidence in the leader and be motivated toward the vision.

1. Do you have and communicate a strategy that can move your team toward the future vision? (1 = no, not at all; 10 = yes, very much so)

    1 2 3 4 5 6 7 8 9 10

    _____
    _____
    _____

2. Is your strategy systematic, incremental, and comprehensive, with clear steps for fulfilling the vision? (1 = no, not at all; 10 = yes, very much so)

    1 2 3 4 5 6 7 8 9 10

    _____
    _____
    _____

3. Think further about your strategy by answering these questions:

    (a) What's *right* about the strategic plan, and how will I capitalize on it?

    _____
    _____
    _____

    (b) What's *wrong* about the strategy, and how will I correct it?

    _____
    _____
    _____

    (c) What's *missing* in the strategy, and how will I create or supply it?

    _____
    _____
    _____

    (d) What's *confusing* about the strategy, and how will I clarify it?

    _____
    _____
    _____

Active Resistance

Resistance will always accompany change. But if the driving forces (discontent, vision, strategy) are greater than the resistance, *change will happen.*

Equipping leaders will therefore focus on increasing these driving forces while lowering resistance. Attention needs to be given to both sides of the equation.

Resistance may come in the form of passive-aggressive behavior, fear, entrenched habits, a feeling of lost significance, questioning the real impact of the change, confusion about the future (especially when the vision isn't clear), confusion about roles, and uncertainty on how to make the change (especially when the strategic plan is lacking).

1. How much resistance do you anticipate as you shift toward a gift-based ministry team with greater effectiveness in equipping leadership? (1 = no resistance at all; 10 = a lot of resistance) Explain your answer.

1   2   3   4   5   6   7   8   9   10

_____

_____

_____

2. What do you anticipate to be the three greatest points of resistance as you shift toward a gift-based ministry team with greater equipping leadership effectiveness? Use this chart to identify the source and form of the resistance, plus the actions you'll take.

Source of Resistance	Form of Resistance	Action Step
1.		
2.		
3.		

Critical Questions within the Change Process

Four critical questions need to be asked and monitored as you move through the change process.

1. For the changes you're seeking to make, what are the implications—both good and bad, real and perceived?

For example,

- Will someone's position or role in the ministry change?

- Will the ministry be structured and organized differently?

- Will a specific ministry program or activity be redirected toward different goals, or even done away with completely?

- Are there any financial implications?

- Will certain volunteers or staff members be asked to do more (or less) than they were doing previously?

_____

_____

_____

Some of the implications of change are clearly good; others will be seen as bad. Some of the implications are real; others only perceived. Either way, they need to be identified. In this way, you can anticipate the reactions of those who are affected and work in ways to demonstrate care and concern.

2. Who's being affected?

List the names of those who will be most affected by the implications you just identified. This is especially important to those for whom the change will have a negative effect (either real or perceived).

_____

_____

3. How are they being affected?

What are the specific effects of the change? What will actually change?

_____

_____

4. What's your "pain plan"?

Experts in change management often suggest coming up with a "pain plan" to help those who will be negatively affected by the change. It means addressing people's cares and concerns so they remain fully committed to the ministry while the change is implemented and they are working through their personal transitions.

_____

_____

_____

If the desired change is truly from the Lord, the leader who intentionally and skillfully manages people through their transitions will not only be successful, but will also equip his or her followers in the process. Managing the change process to the benefit of one's followers is at the heart of being an equipping leader.

Implementing the Change Process

Use this exercise to be better aligned with the four major steps identified earlier for embracing the change process.

Understanding these dynamics isn't sufficient to create the kind of change God may be calling you to make. His ways are not our ways. Some changes may seem right to us, yet lead to disappointment. It's not by our own influence or strength that real change in the church happens, but by His Spirit (Isa. 55:9; Prov. 14:12; Zech. 4:6).

We need to ask the Holy Spirit for His wisdom. If we're lacking wisdom, we just need to ask (James 1:5).

The change process outlined below will help you find God's anointing for your role as an equipping leader. It will also help you discern the changes *He* wants to make in you, in your ministry, and in your church.

Pray Fervently

Pray fervently to access God's presence and power.

- *Pray for the Spirit's work.* The Spirit of God moves in response to prayer. To bring about change, we need the power of the Holy Spirit. Change brought about on a human level is different from the change brought about by God. We don't want to be guilty of "tinkering" with the church. It's not *our* church; it's *His*—the *body of Christ.* Personally pursue God in prayer about your role and the ministry changes needed to function more biblically. Pray, "Come, Holy Spirit." Then wait … listen … obey.

- *Confess.* The Spirit may bring to mind unreconciled relationships, selfish desires, broken promises, unrepented sin, and other things that hinder His full anointing on your life and ministry. As a leader, you may need to confess things like ignorance, failing to equip, leadership abuse, using people, or neglect. You may need to seek forgiveness from those you report to, work with, or serve. Offer a sincere confession to the Father by agreeing with the Spirit, so that His presence and power can flow unhindered through your life. Seek forgiveness.

- *Repent.* When you've confessed and agreed with God, your action step is repentance—turning away from any sinful thoughts, behaviors, and patterns. Refuse to repeat the pattern. Recommit your ways to the Lord.

1. How are you praying for your ministry?

_____

_____

_____

2. Remember that you have an enemy—one who is committed to your failure and demise. The Devil is seeking those whom he can destroy (1 Peter 5:8). But God has provided the church with people who are gifted in intercession. Their prayers can form a hedge of protection around you and your ministry.

   List here the names of five people who are passionate about prayer and who would consider a commitment to pray for your ministry and the desired changes. Then invite them to pray for your ministry.

   (1)

   (2)

   (3)

   (4)

   (5)

3. What needs to be confessed, and who are the people or groups that should hear your change of heart? Record your answers here.

What needs to be confessed and forgiven?	Who needs to hear it?

Teach the Word

Any changes God is calling you to make will always be clearly evidenced in Scripture. If you can't find biblical principles and teachings that apply to what *you* want to do, you'll lack the power of God. When you teach the Word as the basis for change, people will understand that what you're leading them to isn't your idea, but God's (Rom. 12:2). The Word can generate healthy discontent as people understand God's will for them. The Word can offer the clear vision for a desirable future to give hope. The Word can guide our steps and be a light to our feet (Ps. 119:105).

4. What biblical teachings give evidence that the changes you seek are from God? List some appropriate passages you can use to help people embrace the change. (For example, Eph. 4:11–16; 1 Cor. 12—14; Rom. 12:1–8)

_____

_____

_____

Lead by Example

There's something very true about the phrase "More is caught than taught." However, both information and modeling are necessary. Each colors how the vision is understood and will be embraced.

Leading by example is clear in Scripture. Jesus called us to be like Him (Luke 6:40). And Paul offers himself as a model (1 Thess. 1:5–6; 2 Thess. 3:7; 1 Tim. 4:12). Likewise, you are a model to your team. You cannot underestimate the significant influence you have on those around you.

Equipping leaders who are modeling the behaviors they're teaching will …

- *train* equippers to equip.

- *equip* servers to serve.

- *affirm* and *reward* those who equip.

- *affirm* and *reward* those who serve.

5. How are you currently leading by example?

    _____

    _____

    _____

6. What are some additional ways you can embrace and demonstrate leading by example?

    _____

    _____

    _____

Create a Vehicle

When you've completed the first three steps (pray, teach, lead), you're left with the *how*. How will you ensure that these things will be applied and lead to life change? It requires some *vehicle* or method of approach to put everything together. Systems provide the vehicle to implement new values.

This is where many leaders fall short. They move too quickly with prayer, teaching, and leading without a delivery system to ensure ministry team application. They fail to create a vehicle to get them there.

7. What is the right vehicle for implementing this change, and how will you use it?

    _____

    _____

    _____

Ways to Sabotage the Changing Phase

Change is required when we move from program planning and event coordinating to actually equipping people. But the leaders driving this change can sabotage the process.

Ask yourself the following questions, and circle your answers. Then indicate any appropriate action steps you will take.

1. When there's sufficient discontent, do you verbalize it in order to bring about change? *Yes / Somewhat / No*

Action step:

_____

_____

_____

2. Do you have a compelling vision? *Yes / Somewhat / No*

Action step:

_____

_____

_____

3. Do you have a vision that addresses the discontent that is present?
Yes / Somewhat / No

Action step:

_____

_____

_____

4. Do you have a working strategy designed to fulfill the vision? *Yes / Somewhat / No*

Action step:

_____

_____

_____

5. Do you address groups who vocally resist needed changes for self-serving reasons?
Yes / Somewhat / No

Action step:

_____

_____

_____

6. Do you demonstrate the patience needed to persevere through the change process?

Yes / Somewhat / No

Action step:

_____

_____

_____

7. Do you focus on the large number of "undecideds"? *Yes / Somewhat / No*

Action step:

_____

_____

_____

8. Do you manage the change process? *Yes / Somewhat / No*

Action step:

_____

_____

_____

9. Do you recognize when a ministry team member needs to make a change or transition, and do you take the initiative to talk to him or her about it? *Yes / Somewhat / No*

Action step:

_____

_____

_____

10. Do you offer to open the door to a new ministry opportunity when you have to close another door for one of your team members? *Yes / Somewhat / No*

Action step:

_____

_____

_____

11. Do you make changes to your calling, connecting, coaching, or changing phases based on the reasons people give for leaving your ministry? *Yes / Somewhat / No*

Action step:

_____

_____

_____

Fork in the Road

FORK IN THE ROAD

If you have developed and implemented a strategic plan where the steps are doable and a healthy process is being sustained, then continue on.

If you need more of an understanding on the development of a basic strategic plan for your ministry, then go to Getting More "H."

PAGE 247 → "Making Strategic Changes"

WELCOME BACK!

Prayer and Action

Take a moment to talk to the head of the church. Acknowledge once more His lordship over you, over your ministry team, and over His church.

Ask how changing can increase your effectiveness and better equip the members of your team.

Write out your thoughts.

_____

_____

_____

_____

_____

 Next Steps

Fear Factors

Now that you've completed session 6, it's time to face your fears. In these Next Steps, consider what keeps you from being the equipping leader God has called you to be.

Since God has made His strategy so clear, why don't most leaders organize the church to function according to spiritual gifts, ministry passions, and equipper-server distinctives?

Here are some of the more common fear factors that keep leaders from adopting this biblical strategy:

1. *I'd lose my position.* Some see the personal implications and are troubled. For example, senior pastors who have primarily serving gifts would need to reevaluate their role, since they're functioning in a position that requires primarily equipping gifts. The same is true for anyone in a leadership position.

2. *It's too much of a hassle.* Some feel that the changes needed are just too difficult to apply. They realize that change will require new ways of thinking and new patterns of behavior that many people would likely resist. It seems like too much of a bother.

3. *It's too huge.* Others find the institutional implications to be overwhelming. Many structures and groups would come under scrutiny to determine their function in a gift-based ministry model. Many things would have to take on new purpose. The implications of change are too complex.

4. *We'd have to admit we've been doing it wrong.* Some question whether this biblical strategy is really necessary. If God really wanted it done differently, why haven't we

heard about it before? Hasn't the way we've organized the church worked just fine for years?

5. *Would it really change anything?* A few aren't sure this strategy would make any fundamental difference. Sure, things might *look* different—but only on the surface.

Got Fear?

1. At this point in experiencing leadershift, what's your greatest fear factor? Is it one of those we just mentioned, or something else?

   _____

   _____

   _____

2. Is your fear more about the organizational changes or about the transitions you'll have to go through personally?

   _____

   _____

   _____

3. How will you address this fear?

   _____

   _____

   _____

4. What scriptures will you draw support from?

   _____

   _____

   _____

Overcoming Fears

The truth is, we *are* to do gift-based, passion-driven ministry (1 Cor. 12:1). It *will* bring about noticeable differences in you, in your ministry, and in the church at large (1 Peter 4:10). Being aligned with God's design enables us to be faithful, fruitful, and fulfilled in the works of service He has created and called us to carry out (Eph. 2:10).

Consider some of the personal and ministry benefits:

- more enthusiasm

- greater participation

- reduced burnout

- increased giving

- more loyalty

- increased fruitfulness

- deeper faithfulness

- added fulfillment

- God is made famous

Bringing about such a thriving church community is the very reason God gave us spiritual gifts.

Our hope is that this Application Guide has been a worthy vehicle for you to better understand your role as an equipping leader—and how to *be* such a leader.

Leaders who embrace God honoring change will overcome their fears.

Jesus was the ultimate example of an equipping leader. What made Him that leader was His willingness and ability to follow the Father. In His earthly ministry, Jesus stated that He did what He saw the Father do, and He said what He heard the Father saying. To the degree that you seek, see, and follow the Holy Spirit, you'll be a loved and honored equipping leader too.

As a result of completeing the *Experiencing LeaderShift Application Guide*, you'll never view leadership the same again. You've made a paradigm shift—a *leadershift*—because you've been experiencing it through this vehicle.

Now, walk worthy of the calling to which you have been called (Eph. 4:1).

Part Three

DOING MINISTRY TOGETHER

By now you realize just how much God wants His people to do ministry together. Through this Application Guide, we trust you're becoming the equipper God has called you to be. Now you're ready for the next step—bringing this truth to the team of people you lead.

To assist you with this, we've created *Experiencing LeaderShift Together*. This curriculum is specifically designed for you to use with your team members so that you all share common understandings and language concerning ministry.

Experiencing LeaderShift Together will help you build your team, as members discover their zones of God's anointing, identify their roles as equippers or servers, and learn to relate to one another as teammates.

So let us encourage you to make plans now to Experience LeaderShift Together.

GETTING MORE

Section A

TWO APPROACHES:
SELF-STUDY AND LEADER-LED

You can take two approaches with the *Experiencing LeaderShift Application Guide*: Self-Study and Leader-Led. Having both of these approaches allows participants to receive quality leadership training in a format that is most helpful for them. Every leader in your church or parachurch ministry can receive identical training. In this way, your leaders develop common understandings concerning ministry and possess a common language for discussing it.

No matter which approach you're taking, we strongly recommend that you read the book, *Experiencing LeaderShift*, before using this Application Guide.

Self-Study Approach

If you're going through this Application Guide on your own, you can simply move at your own pace. However, we do encourage you to commit to a regularly scheduled time and set a goal for its completion.

The best time(s) in my schedule to work through the *Experiencing Leadershift Application Guide* is: (list days and times)

_____

_____

Start Date:_____   Completion Date: _____

Leader-Led Approach

There are several advantages to using the Leader-Led Approach: You can encourage and be encouraged by others who are journeying with you. You can ask questions and discuss the application of what your learning. You can hold one another accountable for your participation. You can wrestle with the implications of what you're learning in the church or ministry overall.

If you're leading others through this guide, you can control the process and adjust the times to allow for the kind of interaction you desire. Here are a few suggested guidelines for maximizing the fruitfulness of this study:

1—Use the DVDs.

2—Schedule the times for each session based on your group's size and the degree of interaction you desire. Make adjustments as necessary to the suggestions given in this book (which are based primarily on the Self-Study Approach).

3—Make sure all the participants are writing down their thoughts, insights, and action steps. This guide serves as a map for their journey. The exercises, assessments, and assignments, in addition to the teaching, are intended to further everyone's understanding of the covered topics.

Ask everyone to consider making a covenant to this journey. A covenant is a promise made to God, or to another in the presence of God. The purpose is to reveal your commitment to each other, for mutual benefit.

Together is better, so have the entire group consider the covenant. (Some may find this difficult and choose to withdraw from the process.)

This can be a tremendous opportunity to build your own team as you lead them through the process.

Here's a possible covenant:

Covenant

Experiencing leadershift is truly my desire. Before God, and before others in this group, I commit to the following:

___ I will pray and seek the Holy Spirit's guidance for my life and ministry.

___ I will create and protect the time needed for completion of the *Experiencing LeaderShift Application Guide.*

___ I will watch each of the DVD segments at the appropriate time.

___ I will complete all of the application exercises to the best of my ability and understanding.

___ I will share what is being learned with the members of my ministry team to assist them in being faithful, fruitful, and fulfilled, and in making God famous.

Your signature: _____

Date: _____

Witness: _____

Witness: _____

A Typical Leader-Led Session

• Greeting/prayer

• Catching up:

"Since we last met, what have you done to apply what you're learning?"

"What has been working?"

"What has been confusing or challenging?"

"What have you been hearing from God about your leadership?"

• As a team leader, cast a vision for this study. (Do this each time you meet.)

- Watch part 1 of this session's DVD segment.

- Reflections

  Your purpose here is to get your group members' initial feelings and thoughts about the DVD segment. Give everyone a few minutes to write down their responses to the questions; then discuss these with the group.

- Application Zone

  Your purpose here is to have them work through the teaching specifically and practically as it relates to their leadership role on a ministry team. Be sure they have time to properly work through the exercises before discussing them as a group. Watch to see that people are actually making the applications, not just engaging in conversation about them.

  (*Option:* End here. If your time is limited, the rest of this session could be covered the next time you meet, making it two sessions instead of one.)

- Watch part 2 of this session's DVD segment.

- Reflections (as before)

- Application Zone (as before)

- Prayer and Action

  Your purpose here is to have them pause to see if they're gaining insights or being prompted by the Holy Spirit to take some specific actions.

- End the session with prayer.

- Be sure to direct them to the Next Steps. These are more applications to be completed individually as "homework" before your group meets again and moves into the next session. *They're not optional.*

(DL)

MINISTRY STRUCTURES:

INSTITUTIONAL AND BIBLICAL

The way churches are structured affects how they function and may prevent them from experiencing the degree of success desired.

As we saw in session 1, the organizational structure of most churches is made up of four primary components. We have outlined two organizational structures under the headings—Institutional and Biblical. The following chart (which you saw in session 1) gives a side-by-side overview of each.

Experiencing LeaderShift, chapter 6

Institutional Structure	Biblical Structure
Board *Led* • The board focuses primary attention on matters of administration (facilities, finances, personnel, etc.). • Board members have significant decision-making authority with minimal ministry leading responsibility.	**Board *Protected*** • The board is responsible for the ministry of the Word and prayer (Acts 6:1–7). • Members are responsible to protect the unity and purity of the church (Heb. 13:17). • They're accountable for the church's influence—fulfillment of the Great Commission (Matt. 28:19–20).
Staff *Serving* • The staff plans programs and coordinates events to meet the needs of the congregation. • The staff has significant responsibility for the work of ministry (leading their program) with minimal decision-making authority.	**Staff *Led*** • The staff is responsible to equip the saints for the work of service (Eph. 4:11–12). • Staff members have appropriate authority and responsibility, with accountability.
Congregation *Served* • The congregation focuses on having its own needs met. • Members respond as consumers and critics of the board and staff.	**Congregation *Serving*** • The congregation contributes to the work of service through gift-based, passion-driven ministry (Eph. 4:11–12; 1 Cor. 12:1).
World *Ignored* • Those outside the church are unaffected and disinterested.	**World *Served*** • As recipients of the church's service, those outside the church find God in and through the body of Christ (John 13:35; Luke 10:30–37; Matt. 28:19–20).

What follows is more explanation of these two models.

The Institutional Model

- Board *led*

  The board is mostly made up of laypeople with significant decision-making authority but minimal ministry responsibility. The members usually meet once a month for a few hours. Their overall focus tends to be on administration. The majority of their time together is spent on operational matters such as budget, operations, buildings, personnel, and other "business"-related issues.

- Staff *serving*

   Staff members are those who are hired by the church and paid for their service. They usually carry significant ministry responsibility with only minimal authority (the board has most of the authority). The staff members are primarily focused on developing programs and events that meet the needs of the congregation. That's what they're paid for.

- Congregation *serving*

   The congregation responds as consumers and critics of the board and staff. The primary focus of the members of the congregation is having their own needs met. They attend events and provide a critique of how well they feel the staff and board are doing in meeting their needs. Many are not actively participating or engaging in the church's development. And they'll leave the church if, as consumers, they feel their needs aren't being met.

- World *ignored*

   Because the Institutional Church Board and Staff are focused on meeting the needs of the existing congregation, and because the congregation is focused on their own experience, the world surrounding the Institutional Church is all-but ignored.

The Biblical Model

- Board *protected*

   In this model, the board has the responsibility of protecting the church. It is called upon to guard the unity and purity of the

fellowship. It is also accountable for the fulfillment of the Great

Commission though the life of the church.

The New Testament's "job description" for elders speaks of shepherding, guarding, and teaching. These are their functions. But it's also clear that God is much more concerned about *who* they are—*character* matters most to the Lord of the church.

Boards should be focused on the greater issues of prayer, church discipline, doctrinal purity, and fulfilling the Great Commission through the Great Commandment.

- Staff *led*

    The staff is primarily responsible for the "*equipping* of the saints for

    the work of service." Staff members equip with intentionality. They

    have appropriate authority and responsibility, with accountability.

Staff may be paid or not paid, full-time or part-time. In the biblical model of ministry, "staff" is defined simply as those having a primary role of equipping servers to serve, or of developing gift-based, passion-driven ministry teams.

Those on staff aren't there simply because they've been ordained or formally educated. Rather, they're qualified to be an equipping staff person because of godly character, proven faithfulness, missional understanding, giftedness, and ministry competence.

- Congregation *serving*

    In this model, the people of God are being faithful, bearing fruit,

    and experiencing fulfillment in ministries that are making God

    famous. They're serving according to their ministry passions and

    spiritual gifts. They're focused primarily on serving. Congregations

    are equipped contributors to the work of ministry—not consumers

    or critics.

- World *served*

    The world takes notice as the church's missional ministries penetrate
    the community at its points of greatest need. Those in the surrounding
    community see Christ's hands and feet in their midst, and they hear
    His voice through the lives of His followers. As recipients of grace,
    love, and service, the world is drawn to God through the body of
    Christ. The lost discover their lostness and find the Christ they've
    longed for.

Section C

PROGRAMS AND VALUES

In many churches, ministry programs exist unto themselves ("silos") for the purpose of successfully accomplishing their individual mission. As a result, what happens in one ministry program has little impact on what happens in another ministry program.

Programs can be defined by the following 3 characteristics …

- they speak to a specific audience.

- they focus on meeting specific needs.

- they last for a specific season in people's lives.

To repeat the example given in session 1, the children's program is obviously for children, addressing their needs as children. When they're no longer children, that program is no longer for them. The same is true of the singles program, the youth ministry, a new believers' class, etc. Such programs in the church serve many good purposes.

There's nothing wrong with a program. Programs are good. They meet real needs in people's lives. But, programs are different from values.

In your church, would you say *worship* is a program or a value? Is *prayer* a program or a value? What about *giving?* All of these should be a value in every church. There's teaching on their importance, and there's often an expectation that these things will be practiced in the life of each follower of Christ and in every ministry.

Some churches will send a team to a nursing home to provide a worship service. Why? Because for these churches, *worship* is a value—and if you can't come to the church, the church will bring worship to you.

Perhaps you take an offering in your children's ministry program. If so, it's not usually because you need each child's quarter, but rather because you want to teach children the value of regular giving. *Giving* is a value.

Values can be defined by the following three characteristics …

- they are for everyone.

- they reflect God's will for His people.

- they are to be applied and lived out for a lifetime.

Programs serve as vehicles to communicate and instill values.

Owning a Value

When you "own" a value, these things are true:

- *You're intellectually convinced.* You see the biblical teaching and believe it to be true. You know you're to obey. There is no doubt about God's will as stated in His word.

- *You're experientially engaged.* You organize your ministry around it. The way you treat people and do ministry reflects your commitment to the value.

- *You're emotionally persuaded.* This goes beyond your intellect or behavior to reveal your heart. If you're *wholeheartedly* (not halfheartedly) committed to this value, then you'll be able to persuasively speak about it with others. They'll see your conviction and be energized.

If you really own the value, all three of these must be personally evident in your ministry.

For example, if you're intellectually convinced but not experientially engaged, your life won't reflect the value. *Stated* values aren't always *lived* values.

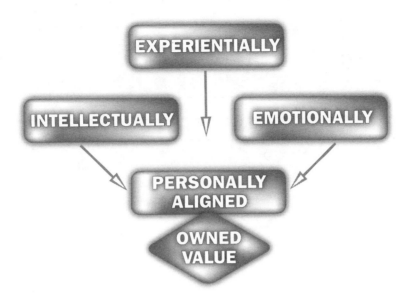

Why Is This Important?

Many leaders and ministry workers see gift-based, passion-driven ministry as simply another *program* in the church. As such, the impact of this truth is minimal in the life of the church.

1. If gift-based, passion-driven ministry isn't owned as a value (as it should be), where's the breakdown? Is it in …

   __ intellectual conviction?

   __ experiential engagement?

   __ emotional persuasion?

2. What needs to be lifted up, taught, or aligned to make this a value in the life of the church or organization?

   _____

   _____

   _____

3. What actions steps do you need to take to truly own the value of gift-based, passion-driven ministry?

_____

_____

_____

PERSONAL MINISTRY ALIGNMENT

If you're primarily an equipper but you're in a serving position, or you're primarily a server but you're in an equipping position, you'll find it difficult to have a successful ministry. When we're in positions that fail to reflect God's design of us, we need to take the initiative to find a position where we can be faithful, fruitful, and fulfilled to the greatest degree.

Here are several steps you can take:

1. Talk to your ministry leader about what you've learned about your equipper-server quotient. Explain your concerns. Your goal here is to begin a discussion about how to find a role that enables you to better fulfill your calling.

   Note: Ministry leaders who haven't been through *Experiencing LeaderShift* or a ministry such as *Network* may not fully understand and appreciate what you want to work through with them. They may attempt to talk you into staying in your position in their ministry, simply because you're "needed." Be prepared to graciously speak the truth in love. Also seek the counsel of those who do understand your situation.

2. Complete some personal assessments, such as …

   • the three assessments in session 1—Personal Success, Ministry Success, and Leadership in the Zone of God's Anointing.

- *What You Do Best in the Body of Christ* and the *Network* course (at www. brucebugbee.com).

3. Pursue the ministries that allow your heart to express its passion. Explore the available ministry positions that reflect your spiritual gifts. If you're an equipper, find an equipping position; if you're a server, find a serving position. If none exist in the ministry where you want to serve—can one be created? If not, explore another ministry.

4. Be responsible when making a ministry change. Growth and alignment is a process. Be sure you're working with your leader and ministry team to make a timely change in your ministry or role. Sometimes it can happen immediately. Sometimes it may require weeks or months in order to find and train someone to replace you. Honor those around you as you pursue God's calling on your life.

5. Monitor your faithfulness, fruitfulness, and fulfillment in the new ministry role. Seek counsel. Continue to make adjustments as the Holy Spirit leads you.

IDENTIFYING A TEAM FIT

(KEY QUESTIONS)

The following questions are designed to provide ministry leaders with enough information to assess the suitability of a potential equipper or server based on how God equipped them to serve:

- character

- spiritual maturity

- ministry fit

- team fit

These are sample questions; you can also create your own. Prayerfully select the questions that are the most helpful and appropriate. Circle or underline the numbers of the questions you decide to use.

As you use these questions with potential equippers or servers, it's important to remind them there are no right or wrong responses. Your goal is simply to better understand how God has created and called them.

Character

(Ability to manage one's life)

1. If I were to ask your spouse or best friend what two or three things they value most about you, what would they say?

2. What personal weaknesses seem to hold you back from being the person you desire to be?

3. Tell me about a time in your life when you've failed. How did you recover from that setback?

4. Who do you consider your closest friends? Why are you drawn to them?

5. Tell me about a time in the recent past when you've been hurt. How did you handle the situation?

6. How do you like to be led and given feedback?

7. How would you describe the current condition of your home life?

What other questions could you ask to determine character? List them here:

8. _____
   _____
   _____

9. _____
   _____
   _____

10. _____
    _____
    _____

Spiritual Maturity

(The experience of walking in the Spirit)

1. Please share with me how you came into a personal relationship with Christ.

2. How do you maintain your relationship with the Lord in an ongoing way?

3. Have you ever fallen away from the Lord? What brought it on? What brought you back?

4. How do you think Christ would describe your current relationship with Him?

5. Have you ever been discipled?

6. Are you in a small group? Tell me about that experience.

7. How long have you been attending the church? How do you view membership?

8. Is this church doing or teaching anything you're uncomfortable with?

What other questions could you ask to determine spiritual maturity?

9. _____
_____
_____

10. _____
_____
_____

11. _____
_____
_____

Ministry Fit

(Alignment of spiritual gifts, ministry passions, personal style)

1. What do you understand your ministry passion to be?

2. Why are you interested in this ministry?

3. What are your top three spiritual gifts?

4. How have the spiritual gifts you identified been affirmed to you?

5. Ideally, what percent of your time each week would you prefer to work with people? And what percent of the time would you like to be doing tasks?

6. Are you more comfortable in the role of creating, developing, managing, or doing?

What other questions could you ask to determine ministry fit?

7. _____
_____
_____

8. _____
_____
_____

9. _____
_____
_____

Team Fit

(Affinity among team members)

1. What do you most enjoy doing in your spare time?

2. Would you say you prefer working independently or on a team? Why?

3. When you participate in something that requires a group effort, what role do you typically play?

4. What do you do when you feel stressed or overwhelmed?

5. What does accountability in ministry mean to you?

6. When you disagree with those in authority or leadership over you, what do you do?

7. In what other ways are you (and your spouse) relationally connected in this church?

What other questions could you ask to determine team fit?

8. _____
_____
_____

9. _____
_____
_____

10. _____
_____
_____

GETTING A VISION

A Ministry Vision

A vision is a description—a picture—of a desired future. It provides an answer to the question, "What will this ministry look like when the mission is being accomplished?"

Put another way, the vision is a destination. It's the place you intend to go as a result of fulfilling your mission.

For a biblical framework for this, let's look at Matthew 28:19–20, where Jesus states His mission for His disciples:

> Go therefore and make disciples of all the nations, baptizing them in the name
> of the Father and the Son and the Holy Spirit, teaching them to observe all that
> I commanded you; and lo, I am with you always, even to the end of the age.

Had Jesus gone on to further articulate this vision, He could have stated what we read in Acts 2:42–47, where we find a description of what took place as a result of that mission being accomplished: A community of people was formed who "were continually devoting themselves to the apostles' teaching and to fellowship, to the breaking of bread [worship] and to prayer." As a result of such devotion, the power of God was on display among them: "Everyone kept feeling a sense of awe; and many wonders and signs were taking place" (v. 43). They were sharing all that they had with one another so that no one was left without (vv. 44–45). They were united in their commitment and met regularly together for fellowship (v. 46). And they worshipped the Lord together and received favor from those in the surrounding community in such a way that many were being added to their community (v. 47).

Had Jesus provided this description in advance, He would have been casting a vision.

We trust that you have a clear understanding of the mission of your ministry. (If not, we strongly encourage you to stop and do the necessary praying, thinking, and discussing to identify and articulate it.)

With your mission clearly identified and articulated, you now need to answer this question: "What will this ministry look like when the mission is being accomplished?" Write a description. Draw a picture using words. The clearer, the better; the more specific, the more beneficial.

While the people you're calling to join your team need to know the mission of the ministry, it's the vision that will really capture their imagination. The casting of a vision is at the heart of calling.

A Personal Vision

With the ministry vision clearly cast, all potential team members need to know, "What role can I play in the fulfillment of this vision?" They want to know what contribution you believe God has equipped them to make toward the fulfillment of this vision. The answer becomes their *personal* vision.

The equipping leader is one who casts a personal vision to each potential teammate, so that each one clearly understands the role and significance of his or her contribution. Remember, you are *not* recruiting people to fulfill a responsibility; you're inviting them to embrace a calling to make a contribution in fulfillment of a mission and vision. That's where the equipping process begins.

A person's passion connects to …

the ministry leader's vision, which contributes to …

the church's mission, which advances …

God's kingdom in the local and global community.

God's Vision: No More and No Less

Toward the end of Jesus' earthly ministry, He offers a prayer to His Father in John 17. In this prayer, Jesus says He has accomplished the work the Father gave Him to do (John 17:4). The implication is that He accomplished no more than that, and no less.

In this same prayer, Jesus also says that He spoke the words the Father gave to Him to speak (John 17:8). Again the implication is, no more and no less.

Jesus spoke the words God gave Him to speak, and He did the works God gave Him to do. *No more and no less.*

Let me provide an analogy. A leader hears the Holy Spirit telling him to take his ministry across the river. Then the leader stands before his people and says, "God is calling us to move across the river. So, let's get to work and cut down some trees, build boats and rafts, and obey the Lord." With excitement the people turn to obey, but to their dismay, they don't see any trees. They now question if their leader has really heard from God, because they can't do what they've been told.

The leader should have said, "God has told me that our ministry is to move across the river"—and stopped there. Because he assumed he knew *how* God wanted them to get there, he connected that to the "vision," and people questioned his leadership. Had he just said what God told him, then the leaders and the people would have asked the *how* question. They would have discovered the best way for them was to use the resources they had, which was iron ore. They could build metal boats!

In this story, God just said *where*, not *how*. Sometimes God says more, sometimes less. Our responsibility is to simply cast the vision He has given us—no more, no less.

When God has given you, the leader, a vision for a ministry, church, or organization, you want to be sure to communicate what He *has* revealed to you—and leave out what He hasn't. When we add to His vision, or downsize it, we fail to be a faithful steward of the vision He entrusted to us.

A man-made vision will not capture God's Spirit in the heart of a believer. A man-made vision will not kindle the passion in His people. But when you cast a godly vision accurately, you'll draw the people and provision needed to bring it to reality.

MINISTRY MISSION STATEMENTS

It's important to identify in a simple statement the basic purpose or mission of your ministry.

When team members read this ministry mission statement, it should connect with their passion. It will create excitement and energy, and motivate them to participate in the ministry.

You can adopt these statements as your own, or you can adapt them to your specific ministry goals. In either case, a good ministry mission statement should include these two elements:

- how the ministry will glorify God
- how the ministry will edify others

After Hours Crisis Team Ministry—We're committed to being available by phone to those facing a crisis, to provide a safe place for counsel or comfort, or to make an immediate referral for care.

Benevolence Ministry—We're committed to compassionate intervention with listening, understanding, discernment, and tangible mercy in providing financial support to assist individuals and families through their crisis or need.

Bookstore Ministry—We're committed to getting life-changing resources into the hands of those who are seeking and growing toward Christ.

Budget Ministry—We're committed to discipling people in the principles and practice of biblical stewardship.

Building Services Ministry—We're committed to creating a service-oriented atmosphere while maintaining quality facilities, so that whoever enters the building may grow in their understanding of Christ in a distraction-free environment.

Business Office and Accounting Ministry—We're committed to supporting the vision and ministries of the church by helping the church effectively steward its resources.

Children's Ministry—We're committed to creating a child-centered environment to supplement the family in providing an age-appropriate and accurate understanding of who God is, so that in God's timing the child will come to have a personal relationship with Jesus Christ.

Computer Team Ministry—We're committed to providing the information systems and support that enable the ministries of the church to serve with more efficiency and effectiveness.

Decorating Team Ministry—We're committed to providing excellent decorations through caring groups in order to create an atmosphere where relationships can be developed and ministries enhanced.

Defenders Ministry—We're committed to providing answers to the intellectual questions that keep seekers from trusting Christ.

Drama Team Ministry—We're committed to presenting real-life, contemporary drama sketches that create high audience identification, by engaging emotions and heightening awareness of the speaker's topic.

Evangelism: Basic Training Ministry—We're committed to equipping believers in naturally sharing their faith with people they know.

Evangelism Ministry—We're committed to developing believers and assisting those with gifts or passion for helping lost people take the next step in the process that leads to faith in

Christ.

Food Pantry Ministry—We're committed to showing the love of God to the needy in a tangible way by providing food—first to those in the church, and then to those in the community.

Food Service Ministry—We're committed to providing healthy food and excellent decorations through caring groups in order to create an atmosphere where relationships can be developed and ministries enhanced.

Graphics Ministry—We're committed to providing proven and competent graphic designers and a communication support team to creatively enhance life-changing events.

Greeters Ministry—We're committed to reflecting God's love and grace with a friendly, warm, and safe environment void of distraction for seekers and believers, so they can hear God's voice through the events of the service.

Grounds Ministry—We're committed to reflecting the excellence of God by creating and maintaining a negative-free environment for seekers, and a worshipful one for believers.

Hearing Impaired Ministry—We're committed to serving the needs of the hearing impaired so they may grow in fellowship and develop into fully devoted followers of Jesus Christ.

Marketplace Ministry—We're committed to teaching a biblical view of work in order to build healthy households, and to assist individuals in realizing their full potential for meaningful and gainful employment in the marketplace.

Marriage Enrichment Ministry—We're committed to building personally fulfilling, God-honoring marriages.

Marriage Premarital Ministry—We're committed to assessing readiness, offering counseling, and providing mentoring couples for building God-honoring marriages.

Marriage Rebuilders Ministry—We're committed to providing biblical insights and relational support to anyone who has experienced marital breakdown, separation, or divorce, in order to bring them to a resolve that honors God.

Missions—We're committed to providing life-changing experiences by serving people in differing ethnic peoples and economic settings cross-culturally, but not necessarily internationally, while creating more Christlike values in those who serve.

Music Ministry: Band—We're committed to developing a community of talented instrumentalists who desire to honor God by supporting the flow and theme of the service with quality music.

Music Ministry: Choir—We're committed to developing people with a spirit of worship, so that through a community of voices they're able to uniquely enhance the congregational worship experience.

Music Ministry: Orchestra—We're committed to developing a community of talented musicians who desire to honor God by supporting the flow and theme of the service with quality music.

Music Ministry: Vocal Team—We're committed to developing a community of talented vocalists who desire to honor God by supporting the flow and theme of the service with quality music.

Network—We're committed to building up the body of Christ by assisting believers in better understanding who God has made them to be and how they can reflect their passion, spiritual gifts, and personal style in a meaningful place of service in and through the local church.

Nursing Home Ministry—We're committed to caring for aging people by providing quality care and spiritual support that values the individual while attending to their needs.

Pastoral Care: Caseworker Ministry—We're committed to moving an individual or family from a position of crisis to a position of stability in which everyone is taking responsibility for his or her decisions.

Pastoral Care: Funeral and Memorial Ministry—We're committed to providing comfort and support for the families and friends of the deceased, allowing for the expression of legitimate grief and acknowledging the hope made available through Jesus Christ.

Pastoral Care: Hospice Ministry—We're committed to providing quality care and support for those with a chronic or terminal illness.

Pastoral Care: Rainbows Support Group Ministry—We're committed to demonstrating the love of God by affirming the individual worth of each child who's processing the loss (through separation, divorce, or death) of a parent or a significant person in his or her life.

Pastoral Care: Visitation Team Ministry—We're committed to calling upon the sick or injured, bringing Christ's presence with mercy and encouragement as representatives of the church.

Prayer Team Ministry—We're committed to keeping the needs of God's leaders and His people before the throne of grace in believing Jesus when He said that where two or three are gathered in His name, He is there; and when they agree in prayer, it will be done.

Print and Copy Room Ministry—We're committed to reaching people by providing a critical link in multiplying ministry through printed materials.

Prison Ministry—We're committed to creating hope and life-change in those who are separated from society by incarceration, or who are transitioning back into society.

Production Team Ministry—We're committed to responding with technical excellence to the needs of the programming team with a can-do, flexible, and service-oriented attitude in order to impact lives for Christ.

Programming Team: Celebration Arts Ministry—We're committed to honoring God by artistically creating a visual environment to support programmed events.

Programming Team: Lighting Ministry—We're committed to honoring God through technical excellence by creating a visual environment to support programmed events.

Programming Team: Stage Design Ministry—We're committed to honoring God through technical and artistic excellence by creating a visual environment to support programmed events.

Reception Ministry—We're committed to providing a gracious and hospitable greeting for callers and guests, connecting them to the appropriate resources of the church.

Singles Ministry—We're committed to connecting singles in community, meeting their relational and spiritual needs as they become fully devoted followers of Christ.

Small Group Ministry—We're committed to connecting people relationally in groups (four to twelve individuals) for the purpose of growing in Christlikeness, loving one another, and contributing to the work of the church, in order to glorify God.

Sports and Fitness Ministry—We're committed to providing regular attenders a way to connect with members and develop relationships through a variety of sports and fitness programs.

Traffic Team Ministry—We're committed to providing attenders with easy access on and off the church campus with a friendly, service-oriented concern for people and vehicle safety.

Unwed Mothers Ministry—We're committed to providing confidential support to single women who have chosen to honor God by completing their unplanned pregnancies.

Ushers Ministry—We're committed to reflecting God's love and grace with a friendly, warm, and safe environment void of distraction for seekers and believers, so they can hear God's voice through the events of the service.

Vehicle Ministry—We're committed to creating community for relational and spiritual growth out of which God can be worshipped with our gifts and talents to serve those who are in need of a car, car repairs, or ministry transportation.

Visitor Response Team Ministry—We're committed to providing a timely response to the questions guests ask about the church's ministries and beliefs.

Wedding Host Ministry—We're committed to revealing the love and care of Christ by coordinating and assisting families for a God-honoring wedding.

Welcome Room Ministry—We're committed to providing an immediate opportunity for personally interacting with visitors who want to know more about the church, or to discuss their spiritual journey in a safe and nonthreatening environment.

Women's Ministry—We're committed to supporting and equipping women for life and ministry by encouraging them to take the next step in their personal growth (spiritually, relationally, emotionally, physically, intellectually).

Youth: High School—We're committed to modeling a servant attitude while addressing the needs of high school students, creating life change, and leading them to become fully devoted followers of Christ.

Youth: Junior High—We're committed to creating an encouraging, exciting, and safe process through which junior high students can experience life change relationally, emotionally, spiritually, and physically.

MAKING STRATEGIC CHANGES

For developing a strategic plan and delivery system for change, here are three key questions to answer:

1. Where am I? (Current state)

Describe the current condition of your leadership, ministry team, church.

Today, our ministry team is ...

_____

_____

_____

2. Where should I be? (Future vision)

Describe the desired future of your leadership, ministry, church.

In the future, our ministry team will be ...

_____

_____

_____

3. How will I get there? (Strategy)

Describe specific steps you'll take to get from the current state to the future vision.

This is our strategy for getting there …

_____

_____

_____

_____

_____

This is our strategy for getting there …

RESOURCES

Network

Bruce Bugbee and Don Cousins, Zondervan

- Leader's Guide
- Participant's Guide
- DVD Drama Vignettes
- CD PowerPoint, User's Guide, Coach's Guide

Available in Spanish and many other languages

What You Do Best in the Body of Christ

Bruce Bugbee, Zondervan

Available in Spanish and many other languages

Discover Your Spiritual Gifts the Network Way

Bruce Bugbee, Zondervan

Walking with God

Don Cousins and Judson Poling, Zondervan

Available in Spanish and many other languages

Listed materials can be ordered from Bruce Bugbee and Associates at 800-588-8833 or brucebugbee.com.

Here is how you can personally contact Don and Bruce:

Don Cousins—individual coaching, ministry

consulting, training, and speaking

www.doncousins.org

616-396-9625

don.cousins@sbcglobal.net

Bruce Bugbee—leadership assessments, training, and ministry consulting

www.brucebugbee.com

800-588-8833

staff@brucebugbee.com

Section J

DOWNLOADS

Aligning a Ministry Team with Ministry Mission and Vision

Appreciation

Assessing the Equipper's Ministry

Assessing the Server's Ministry

Avoiding Usery

Balanced Teams

Covenant

Equipper-Server Quotient

Identifying a Team Fit (Key Questions)

Implementing the Change Process

Leadership in the Zone of God's Anointing

Leading the Change Process

Making Strategic Changes

Ministry Mission Statements

Ministry Position Description Form

Ministry Structures

Ministry Success

Ministry Team Alignment

People Pockets

Personal Success

Programs and Values

Unsuccessful Servants

Ways to "Put More In"

Ways to Build Teams

Who Are You Equipping to Expand Your Ministry?